FROG
FIELD MANUAL

DOC FROG'S
PHYSICAL TRAINING MANUAL

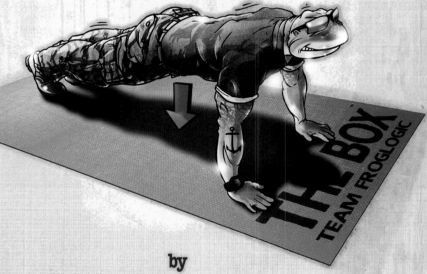

by

David Rutherford
NAVY SEAL
&
BEHAVIORAL TRAINING SPECIALIST

FFMK0001 ISSUED BY
TEAMFROGLOGIC HQ

Froglogic,™ Team Froglogic,™ Doc Frog™ and their logos are trademarks. For more information about Froglogic Concepts, LLC, please visit our website at www.teamfroglogic.com.

Rutherford, David B.

       Froglogic Field Manuals for Kids, vol. 1, DOC FROG'S PHYSICAL TRAINING MANUAL, by David B. Rutherford

ISBN-13: 978-0-9801464-5-5

Printed in the United States of America

First Edition: February 2014

About the Author

David Rutherford is a US Navy SEAL, Combat Paramedic and SEAL Instructor. After traveling the world as a SEAL and then as an International Training Specialist, David discovered his true mission in life, helping kids and adults to live healthy, focused well-balanced lives. Since changing missions from serving in the Navy SEAL Teams to becoming a top motivational speaker, author, radio show host, TV personality, mentor and life coach, David has reached over 2 million people around the world. As a top behavioral training specialist, he hopes to introduce children, parents and educators to the importance of Embracing Fear, Forging Self-Confidence and Living the Team Life. Through his incredibly unique motivational superhero, Doc Frog,™ David teaches youth how to live a healthy lifestyle through physical exercise, proper nutrition, shaping mental focus, spiritual commitment and team oriented living with his Froglogic Concept.

About the Artist

Brian Kalt began scribbling and drawing in the margins of his textbooks, like many youngsters, around the age of 5. He was encouraged by his father to doodle on a regular basis. This led to some extra interest and support from art teachers throughout middle and high school. With some gentle prodding, he made the leap to the University of Florida and fully embraced drawing and oil painting as a major. Since graduating in 1995, he has worked in the apparel industry, supporting licenses from MARVEL to The Rolling Stones. Having the opportunity to participate in the development of this Field Manual has been both challenging and exceptionally rewarding. It is an honor to contribute to such a positive and life-affirming project.

WARNING

The expressed written opinions in this book are based solely on the experiences and teachings of David Rutherford. Please consult your doctor or parent prior to doing any of the exercises in this book. Do not attempt any of the US Navy SEAL exercises without the express approval of your legal guardian. The exercises in this book are basi in nature, but injury may occur if performed incorrectly. This book is intended to help to inspire and motivate kids, parents and educators to live healthy lives.

Froglogic™ Definition:

roglogic™ (frog-lojik), n.v. 1. A motivational philosophy
hat strengthens a person's body, mind and spirit and
erpetually inspires that individual's desire to embrace
ar, forge their Self-Confidence and Live The Team Life.
A three-part motivational training program. (Part 1)
Accepting 5 Life Missions to Embrace Fear and begin
sing your fear as a positive productive piece of motiva-
onal gear. (Part 2) - Accepting 8 Life Missions into
our lifestyle in order to forge your Self-Confidence.
Part 3) - Accepting 4 Life Missions that will ignite your
nderstanding of what it means to live the Team Life.
A concept rooted in the proven successes of over 70
ears of UDT/ Navy SEAL operations, training and elite
festyle performance, expanded by the overall
pecial Operations Mindset.

Preface

Who is Doc Frog™ and why should you listen to him? Doc Frog™ is my creation and I'm a Navy SEAL Medic. Doc Frog™ is a Special Operations Superhero designed to inspire and educate kids to become healthier physically, mentally and spiritually.

When I first started my motivational entertainment company in 2005, Froglogic™ Concepts, LLC, my sole intention was to help children around the world. I wanted to teach them that no matter what negative insurgency they faced, as long as they learned to embrace fear, forge self-confidence and live a Team Life they would be okay. This was and is my mission in life.

Inspired during an actual mission in Afghanistan in 2005, I was called into action to help kids endure the hardships of life and teach them critical lessons learned to persevere in every environment imaginable. After years and years of real world experience, extensive research and development as a top behavioral training specialist, I have discovered the very best ways to educate kids and adults to become better human being

It's paramount that a person must be motivated in conjunction with any form of education in order to have true behavioral changes take place. What better way to

each and inspire kids to forge healthy lifestyle habits
han through the wisdom and actions of a totally awe-
ome, super cool, cartoon character? That's why Doc
rog™ and I want you! We want you to become active
uty members of our motivational training team, Team
roglogic.™ By completing this field manual and accept-
ng the missions within, you will begin shaping the suc-
ess of your future. Embrace Doc Frog's™ high-energy
tyle of motivational fitness to help you begin getting
our body, mind and spirit ready for the battle of life.
Thank you for your support. HOOYAH

David Rutherford
Owner/Creator
Froglogic Concepts, LLC

Dedication

David's Dedication

To Heather. For teaching me that I must eternally focus on keeping my body, mind and spirit strong for those I love most, my teammates.

Brian's Dedication

To Gabriel Richard. Take this manual and make it your own.

FROGLOGIC™

FIELD MANUALS FOR KIDS

DOC FROG'S™
PHYSICAL TRAINING MANUAL

INTRO

Recruit, are you feeling **Froggie**? Well are you? Are you ready to begin using **Froglogic**™ to change your life? Are you fired up to **Embrace Your Fears, Forge Your Self-Confidence** and learn to **Live the Team Life**? Well are you? Me too, let's do it, **HOOYAH!**

My name is **Doc Frog**™ and I'm a **Team Leader** at the **Team Froglogic**™ motivational training company. We are a group of former **Special Operators** and **Motivational Superheroes** who have accepted our mission to help you and your teammates find life-lasting motivation by staying motivated and living healthy lives. <u>Our goal is to train you to defeat the negative insurgency of life,</u> while teaching you the lessons we have learned over the past 100 + years conducting the most extreme missions. Our plan is to share with you the very best motivational training lessons to help you face the greatest challenges in your life.

Mental Note: ✓

Life is hard. You need to recruit and build an awesome team around you in order to realize your dreams and live life to its fullest. Don't ever be afraid to ask your family, close friends or some one you respect to help you achieve your dreams.

Intel Words: ✓

Intel Words — Intel words are words or phrases that will help define motivational ideas and concepts that enable you to achieve any mission you accept.

FFMK0001 ISSUED BY
TEAMFROGLOGIC HQ

Froglogic™ – A way of thinking that perpetually ignites your desire to embrace your fears, forge your self-confidence and live a Team Life. Thinking like a Frogman.

Team Life – A way of living that demonstrates your total commitment towards living a team oriented lifestyle.

Negative Insurgency – The never-ending assault from negative ideas, concepts and people operating in and around your world.

TEAM FROGLOGIC™ wants YOU! I'm recruiting you to become my new Swim Buddy and to help you prepare for Mission:Life. We are dedicated to doing everything we can to help YOU light the fire in your gut and begin living the Team Life. Let us teach you how to be positive, healthy and accept that "The Only Easy Day Was Yesterday." Our team understands how difficult life can be. We've all gone through really tough times. We've all experienced how painful and confusing life can be. After years of operations around the world facing the negative insurgency, we know the truth: alone we fail but together we succeed. No matter what happens in your life, as long as you have a committed team around, you're going to be OK. This is our operating gospel and that's why we encourage you to start Living the Team Life by reading this Field Manual

for Kids. Do it with a parent or other chosen teammate
like your father, mother, brother, sister or best friend.
Together or by yourself you can begin to forge your
body, mind and spirit. HOOYAH!

Intel Words:

Swim Buddy – A person who has your back in the best of
times and worst of times. A person you can count on with
your life.

Mission:Life – Your purpose or dreams that drive you to gro
stronger physically, mentally and spiritually.

Fire in the gut – The burning desire you feel to stay
motivated in the face of all challenges no matter what
the outcome.

The only easy day was yesterday – A Navy SEAL motto
that helps SEALs remember to accept that nothing great in
life comes easy. Hard work is required to become elite.

The first step in our Mission:Life is to introduce you to
the Froglogic Triad. This Triad concept requires you to
focus on all the lessons we teach you about three main
aspects of your life: your Body, Mind and Spirit. These
three ideas make up the truth of who you are. If you
don't focus your efforts on improving your Triad every
day, you will get caught in the undertow of life!

FFMK0001 ISSUED BY
TEAMFROGLOGIC HQ

You must strengthen each aspect of the Triad in order to Embrace Fear, Forge Your Self-Confidence and Live the Team Life. At any point in your life, if you're not focused on strengthening your Triad, any one or all of your fears, lack of self-confidence or bad Team Life can begin to sink your Mission:Life. It's up to you to decide that your ship is steady and your crew, your team, is ready to weather the storm. X

Intel Words:

Froglogic™ Triad – A focused, strong Body, Mind and Spirit.

Recruit, I know that you're under attack. I feel your pain. I too have struggled in life. In fact, there have been plenty of times when I didn't think I was going to make it off the battlefield of life. I felt totally lost swimming alone in one giant ocean of fear. Then one day I decided to change my life. I decided to leave my little hometown pond and join the service and become a Navy SEAL. I knew that I needed to challenge myself in the highest possible way and that I needed to be a part of a team while facing that challenge. I needed to take charge of my own decisions and be accountable for my own success. I found what I was looking for in the SEAL Teams. Going through the most difficult training on the planet taught me that I CAN do so much more than I had ever imagined. As long as I forged my body, mind and spirit and committed to living a Team Life, I discovered I would never feel lost at sea again. It was and is, AWESOME!

After serving the greater good, I made the focused decision to continue serving. I accepted a new mission in life. My mission and the mission of every Operator at Team Froglogic™ is to help you fulfill your Mission:Life. That's right, YOU! Our Mission is to Hammer you into the strongest, healthiest, most squared away Team Froglogic™ Operator ever. We've created an incredible motivational training program designed to get you prepared to endure the hardships of life and then use your experiences to help you achieve your dreams. We've created a self-help series of books called Froglogic Field Manuals for Kids. These manuals are designed to help you Embrace Your Fear, Forge Your Self-Confidence and Live the Team Life. All while you strengthen your body, mind and spirit.

Intel Words:

Operator – A focused, dedicated teammate who pushes himself or herself every day to become better at achieving Mission:Life.

Hammer – The physical, mental and spiritual challenges we face every day. Sometimes we get hammered on purpose through training, and sometimes we get hammered by the negative insurgency.

quared Away™– A feeling that Operators feel when all spects of their lives are focused.

roglogic Field Manuals for Kids– A series of kids' training anuals designed by Team Froglogic that help children nbrace their fears, forge their self-confidence and live the arm Life. All manuals focus on strengthening kids' bodies, inds and spirits through living healthy balanced lifestyles.

n our first Field Manual for Kids, "Doc Frog's Physical 'raining Manual," we focus on your physical training r PT by teaching you how to execute and develop a itness program for yourself, similar to the ones we use n the SEAL Teams. Forging your body is a natural way o start getting big increases in your mental and piritual health. In all Froglogic Field Manuals, we use simple, common sense approach to motivational earning that helps get recruits squared away in their ight against all negative aspects of life. We use Missions to help you organize and understand the earning process. It's our mission to help you strengthen our body, mind and spirit, which in turn will help you eal with trouble at home, at school and with life in eneral. By accepting the easy to use Mission training latform to help guide your strategic development, you vill be on your way to becoming an elite Team Froglogic™ perator!

At the beginning of each Mission, we include a daily nutritional menu to help you and your team get the right fuel for your body. This is because the fuel that goes into your body is critical to your success in becoming an Operator for Team Froglogic. As you move into the meat of the Missions, it's critical to have enough energy to complete the Physical Training or PT. We believe that a strong body enables you to put up a great fight against all the negativity you face in your Mission:Life. Plus a healthy body opens the door to begin getting your mind and spirit ready for battle, too. The Missions in this Manual are specifically designed to build the three critical areas of your health: Body, Mind and Spirit.

So let's get fired up to begin getting squared away. Let's work together, along with your team, to begin to Embrace Your Fears, Forge Your Self-Confidence and Live the Team Life. I'm Doc Frog™ and I'm your new Swim Buddy, so let's get motivated. HOOYAH!

Recruit, achieving mission success means completing this entire Field Manual from start to finish. That means having a total commitment to yourself and your team. Starting what you finish is one of the greatest lessons you can learn as a Team Froglogic™ Operator striving to achieve your dream during Mission: Life.

Doc Frog™
BUDS Class 209

FFMK0001 ISSUED BY
TEAMFROGLOGIC HQ

The Box™

kay Recruits, The Box™ is your mobile PT Platform. This hysical fitness device is part of your gear or kit that eam Froglogic offers in order to get you physically, mentally and spiritually squared away. The idea is that no matter where you are, as long as you have enough pace to roll out The Box™ you can perform your PT. You an PT in your backyard, in your bedroom, in the TV oom or even in your classroom. In my opinion, the est place to PT is outside. Find an awesome place to oll out The Box™ and get your body squared away." Embrace the beauty of the outdoors and the incredible eeling of getting stronger by hammering yourself on The Box today. **HOOYAH!**

—Bring It!

FFMK0001 ISSUED BY
TEAMFROGLOGIC HQ

PT INTEL

Okay Recruits, here's some mission critical PT Intel or Physical Training Intelligence. This information will help you understand, plan and execute the missions challenging you in this Field Manual. It's important you use this Intel before, during and after every mission you accept. Do not blow this information off! Pay attention to every detail and be accountable in performing all required steps to the best of your ability. Now stand by to begin your mission. HOOYAH!

1. **Energy and Fuel** – When you decide to become an elit operator on Team Froglogic, it's important that you provide your body the best possible fuel for the mission you're accepting. This is especially true when partici- pating in any vigorous activity like conducting PT. Listen up Recruits, what you put in your body matters! Don't put junk in the engine. That's why we offer an example of a healthy daily menu at the beginning of every Mission. Make sure you have the right fuel for the mission.

2. **Hydration** – Hydrate or die, it's that simple Recruits. When engaging in vigorous activity your body will sweat. You sweat to cool your engine. If you don't properly provide the engine with the right fluids, your engine is going to crash, period. I've seen it happen a to

ix

f times in environments all around the world. Deserts, ungles, Snowy Mountains, and even in gyms. Your ody needs fluids to conduct all missions. Make sure ou're properly hydrated prior to, during and after very mission you accept. Here is more Intel to help you auge your fluid intake:

> "According to the American College of Sports Medicine, to avoid dehydration, active people should drink at least 16 - 20 ounces of fluid one to two hours before an out-door activity. After that, you should consume 6 to 12 ounces of fluid every 10 to 15 minutes that you are out-side. When you are finished with the activity, you should drink more. How much more? To replace what you have lost: at least another 16 to 24 ounces (2 - 3 cups)."
>
> *Taken from the Cleveland Clinic Website*

. Proper Attire and Gear or Kit – Every mission you articipate in requires a specific type of attire and gear. Vhen I used to jump out of airplanes, I used my Air perations Kit bag filled with my flight suit, parachute, imp boots, oxygen mask, helmet, altimeter, main chute, eserve chute and goggles. When I conducted dive perations I broke out my Dive Ops kit bag. Within that ag is all my attire and gear that I use while conducting ive missions. In order to be a squared away operator you need to have the right Kit for the job. Here is a minimum Gear Kit list for the proper execution of operations within this Field Manual.

- PT Shirt (Doc Frog™ PT Shirt) ✓
- PT Shorts or sweats
- PT Footwear
- Water Bottle (Team Froglogic™ H$_2$O Delivery Apparatus)
- Padding (The Box™) - Some surface material that pads your body against the hard floor
- Doc Frog's Physical Training Manual

Suggested Kit and Mission Enhancements

- A Swim Buddy or Teammates. Nothing better than PTing with your team.
- Motivational Music Delivery Apparatus
- Portable Bluetooth Speaker – Make it LOUD!
- A Doc Frog™ bandana to remove sweat

4. Warm up and stretching – Make sure to spend 5 minutes warming up your joints and muscles prior to performing each Mission in this Field Manual. For more information on a proper warm up please visit www.teamfroglogic.com/training/navy-seal-fitness/warm-up.

5. Discomfort or Pain – This is IMPORTANT Intel. If you or your teammates feel discomfort or pain during any part of you accomplishing your missions in this Field

FFMK0001 ISSUED BY
TEAMFROGLOGIC HQ

Manual, STOP what you're doing Recruit. Assess the situation by evaluating exactly what is going on with your body. Do not ignore what your body is telling you. Do not push through the pain. Do not tough it out and injure yourself. Seek help from someone who can clearly diagnose what is going on with your body. Ask a person who has lots of experience in dealing with injuries resulting from vigorous activity. For example, your parents, your gym teachers, a physical therapist and perhaps even your doctor. It's critical to push yourself, but not to the point of becoming mission ineffective.

. Recovery and Rest – Recruit, it's critical that after every mission you take some time for your body, mind and spirit to recover and rest. Every operation takes a toll on who we are. Now some missions take a bigger toll than others and therefore require a greater amount of time to recover and rest. For these missions, it's important for you to actively participate in your recovery by stretching your body parts after you've completed the PT Schedules. It also helps to stretch before you go to bed at night. Recovery includes eating and drinking the proper nutritional diet and fluids too. Recovery is a critical component of becoming an elite operator. So is rest. Don't think for one minute that the stronger your body, mind and spirit become, the less

rest you need. In fact it's quite the opposite. Rest is a
huge part of being able to complete all the operations
you will conduct in your Mission:Life. HOOYAH

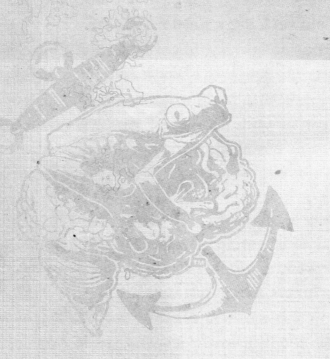

FFMK0001 ISSUED BY
TEAMFROGLOGIC HQ

PT Instructions

Okay Recruit, here's the deal. Pay close attention to the following PT Instructions. This information is designed to help you learn how to perform all the Navy SEAL exercises in this fitness field manual. Once you can execute each exercise or Mission as close to perfect as possible, then you're ready to complete each mission's PT Schedule and Monster Mash at the back of each chapter. Once you've completed a mission PT Schedule and at least one Monster Mash, then you're ready to begin completing the PT Evolutions we have listed at the back of the Field Manual. If you're not sure about a word, phrase or idea, go ahead and check the Glossary in back before moving on. Good luck and stay motivated,

HOOYAH.

Steps: ✓

1. Read the beginning of each Mission. Pay close attention to the Mission Objectives and Mental Notes.

2. Try to use the Nutritional Schedules or menus to help maintain a healthy diet. It's important that you have the right fuel in your body prior to attempting to complete your missions. It's also important to eat properly after you PT as part of your recovery.

3. Be sure to take notes or highlight on your own to remember key points that help you complete each mission and get you fired up.

4. When you reach the "How to do" section of each missio
read the steps all the way through before attempting to
perform the exercise.

5. Once you've read the "How to do" steps, find a good spo
to perform the exercise. Make sure you have all the right
gear for the operation. Place The Box on the ground and
try to execute 5 repetitions of the exercise correctly.
Make sure to have the Field Manual close by in case you
need to read the instructions and visualize me doing the
exercise perfectly.

6. Don't be afraid to use the "Modified" directions if you'r
struggling to do the exercise perfectly. These directions
are listed right after the final step.

7. Write down in the "Debrief" at the end of the mission
any important techniques, tactics or procedures that
helped you complete the exercise.

8. Move on to the next Mission and repeat the previous
steps.

9. After you've completed every mission and each exercis
at least 5 times, make sure you feel comfortable that you'r
performing the exercises safely and correctly. Now it's
time to GO BIG!

10. Time to begin executing the PT Schedules. Starting on
a Monday and continuing throughout the week, pick one
Mission from every Battle and combine the PT Schedules
for all the missions. For instance, choose Push-Ups,
Crunches, Lunges and Jumping Jacks. Now take each
Monday PT Schedule from the missions you've chosen
and combine them into one hard-core PT Evolution for
that day. You must complete all 3 Sets and the repetitions
listed within each column to fully execute the PT Schedules for each mission.

FFMK0001 ISSUED BY
TEAMFROGLOGIC HQ

PT Evolution Example:

Monday	Push-Ups Reps	Crunches Reps	Lunges Reps	Jumping Jacks Reps
Set 1	3,4,6	10,10	5	25
Set 2	5,4,2	10,5	5	25
Set 3	3,4,6	2,4,6	5	10

These PT Schedules and Evolutions will hammer you in the beginning. Don't get frustrated. You've got to learn how to crawl before you walk, and then run. HOOYAH

1. Continue these PT Evolutions until you can complete any 4 combinations of all Mission PT Schedules perfectly. Now you're feeling Froggie, huh? It's time to attempt your first Monster Mash.

2. A Monster Mash is when you combine two days within a Mission PT Schedule. Now add the two days times 4 different Missions from the different Battle Groups. This is the ultimate Navy SEAL Workout. Get fired up, Recruit!

3. Once you've moved into the Monster Mash phase of your PT Training, it's okay to begin using multiple Missions of the same Battle Group. For example, you can choose Push-Ups, Diamond Push-Ups, Lunges and Air Squats. Choose combinations to test your new physical, mental and spiritual strength.

4. If you need help figuring out how to create some PT Evolutions, we have listed a few in the back of the Field Manual to help get you started. Good luck.

15. At any point in your development that you learn some thing new about yourself and your abilities, please don't forget to return to the "Debrief" section of each mission and jot down these critical lessons learned from your experience achieving Mission success.

Note: Try to recruit a swim buddy, family member or teammate to help you complete my Field Manual. There nothing better than getting hammered and strengthenin your body, mind and spirit with a fired up, motivated group of operators. Remember Recruit, always try to Liv the Team Life!

FFMK0001 ISSUED BY
TEAMFROGLOGIC HQ

BATTLE 1: UPPER BODY
MISSION 1: REGULAR PUSH-UPS

DOC FROG

UPPER BODY
MISSION ONE : REGULAR PUSH-UPS

**Mission Objective: To begin building upper bod
strength with one of the oldest and most proven
exercises known in fitness.**

Mental Note:
Strengthening your upper body on a strict
daily schedule will enable you to accomplish
tons of outdoor activities and cool extreme
sports. Don't forget to try to recruit your own
swim buddy to complete all the missions.

Grape Fruit

Nutritional Schedule:

Breakfast –
Two egg whites. A half grapefruit. A glass of lemon water.

Snack 1 –
A handful of grapes and small handful of Goji berries. Glass of
water.

grapes

Gojiberries

Lunch –
An organic chicken sandwich with lettuce, cucumbers, onions
and tomato. On whole wheat bread with mustard.
Big glass of water.

Snack 2 –
Handful of raw almonds and carrots.

I am
what I
☺ eat!!

Dinner –
A Salmon fillet with seasoned vegetables. A glass of Almond Mil

FFMK0001 ISSUED BY
TEAMFROGLOGIC HQ

INTRO

HOOYAH recruits! It's time to listen up. I'm your new swim buddy, Doc Frog. Let's get fired up to begin achieving success in your Mission:Life with your Basic Physical Training or PT. Forget about all those negative thoughts when you wished you were stronger physically, mentally and spiritually. Because together, Living the Team Life, we're going to begin getting you Squared Away™ with learning to love yourself and your team through fitness. This incredible feeling will generate the enduring inspiration you need to push yourself harder physically than you ever have before. I've spent many years pushing myself in the SEAL Teams. The physical strength I forge has a direct impact on the faith I have to be totally committed to my team. A totally healthy body consists of a healthy mind and spirit.

When forging your Froglogic™ Triad it's important to start with your body. That's why it's critical to conduct a fitness routine or some type of hard physical activity for at least 60 minutes a day. Your fitness regimen and activity will guarantee the strong physical foundation you need to continue building your mind and spirit too. There are many ways to approach fitness. What I have found is to embrace KISS or Keep It Simple Stupid. If you begin by developing a simple but

INTRO

effective PT routine or schedule as part of your day, then it's easy to train yourself and your team to have healthy habits and behavior. When regular PT isn't part of your day, everything else is affected. Trust me, without PT other parts of your life will fail. PT needs to be as much a part of you as eating, sleeping and laughing.

Let's get started. There is no better place to start forging your physical strength than with your upper body. Developing your upper body strength has so many benefits towards living a Team Life and fit lifestyle. Think about climbing trees or swimming. Imagine playing basketball or football without using your arms or upper body. How about simply running as fast as you can. All of these body movements require a significant degree of upper body strength that comes from having good control of your chest, shoulders, arms, stomach or Abs, back and of course your legs. Think about how much you use your arms life. How often you are asked to help someone by lending a hand or lifting something to benefit your team. Your upper body strength is crucial to living a productive and active life.

FFMK0001 ISSUED BY
TEAMFROGLOGIC HQ

Where should we start? That's right, PUSH-UPS. Frogmen have been performing basic push-ups for many, many years. From ancient Mesopotamia to modern military Special Operations Training, push-ups have been forging upper body strength for eons. Push-ups are awesome because the exercise strengthens a bunch of commonly used muscle groups. The primary muscles include your chest (pectorals), triceps (triceps brachii), shoulders (deltoid muscle), back and neck (trapezius). However, in order to perform the perfect push-up you must engage your core (abdominal), back and leg muscles. The push-up is a basic exercise that has a huge impact on your upper body strength and can be performed anywhere and any time. Now, let's get fired up and get started.

PUSH-UPS! READY... BEGIN!!

grrrr...

REGULAR PUSH-UPS
How to do a Push-Up:
Step 1. With The Box™ carefully positioned on the ground
place yourself at one end of The Box™ in the Standing
Ready Position. Hands down next to your sides. Feet
shoulder width apart. Positive Attitude, at attention
and ready to hammer yourself.

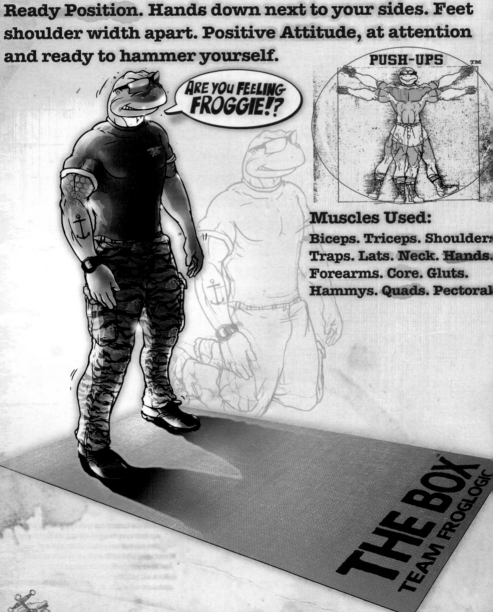

Muscles Used:
Biceps. Triceps. Shoulders.
Traps. Lats. Neck. Hands.
Forearms. Core. Gluts.
Hammys. Quads. Pectoral.

FFMK0001 ISSUED BY
TEAMFROGLOGIC HQ

REGULAR PUSH-UPS

Step 2. Place yourself in the modified Leaning Rest position. Knees down, feet together and toes placed on the Box™ surface. Hands placed palms down and shoulder width apart. Keep your elbows straight.

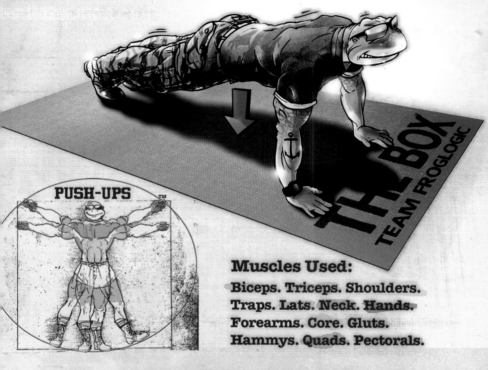

Muscles Used:
Biceps. Triceps. Shoulders. Traps. Lats. Neck. Hands. Forearms. Core. Gluts. Hammys. Quads. Pectorals.

This is the Leaning Rest, Ready or Up position.

Step 3. Using your arms, back and core, lower your chest downward to The Box™. Stop approximately a fist's distance from The Box surface. Make sure to keep your elbows tight against your sides. (Turn the page)

REGULAR PUSH-UPS

Step 4. Using your arms, back and core, lower your chest downward to The Box™. Stop approximately a fist distance from The Box™ surface. Make sure to keep you elbows tight against your sides.

PUSH-UPS™

Muscles Used:
Biceps. Triceps. Shoulders. Traps. Lats. Neck. Hands. Forearms. Core. Gluts. Hammys. Quads. Pectorals.

Step 5. Using your arms, back and activated core, push your body back into the Ready or Up position. Fired up, Recruit, you just did a Wide Grip Push-Up.

Step 6. Repeat again and again according to the amount shown in your Froglogic™ PT Schedule.

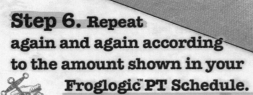

FFMK0001 ISSUED BY
TEAMFROGLOGIC HQ

REGULAR PUSH-UPS

Step 7. When Counting, you should sound off with a loud and thunderous "1" after you have returned to the Leaning Rest or Ready Position. When leading a team, make sure the leader sounds off to direct the group by issuing a preparatory command of "Down" to instruct the team to move down and "Up" to get them up into the Ready Position. Then a sound off with "1!"

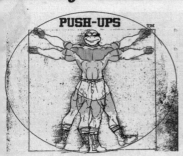

Muscles Used:
Biceps. Triceps. Shoulders. Traps. Lats. Neck. Hands. Forearms. Core. Abs. Gluts. Hammys. Quads. Pectorals.

Modified Push-Ups:

If you begin feeling a little hammered, simply drop your knees down to The Box surface into the modified Leaning Rest. Then drive on. Continue your PT routine and forging your body. Eventually you'll increase your strength and be able to finish all of the PT as listed.

Mental Note:

Part of your mental PT during these exercises is pushing past the frustration of how much time it takes to get stronger. By not quitting, you are building mental muscles that will eventually become bigger than your regular muscles.

REGULAR PUSH-UPS

Enhanced Push-Ups:

Okay Recruits, are you feeling Froggie? If you've forge
your arms, back and Core Abs into raw steel after correctly doing tons of Doc Frog's PT Push-Ups and feel li
a harder challenge, stand by for Feet Raised Push-Ups
Go to DocFrog.com/PT to see Doc Frog's demo and
instructions.

Froglogic™ PT Schedule
Regular Push-Ups:

Reps Sets	Mon	Tues	Wed	Thur	Fri
1	2,4,6	4,6,8	10	5,5,5,5	MONSTER MASH
2	6,4,2	8,6,4	10	3,3,3,3	MONSTER MASH
3	2,4,6	2,4,6,4,2	5,5,5	2,2,2,2	MONSTER MASH

Take a 10 second break between each repetition.
Don't exceed 30 seconds between sets.

DEBRIEF:

Write your positive and negative lessons learned
on these line provided after the completion of each
Mission.

Stay
Focused!!
I can DO it!

FFMK0001 ISSUED BY
TEAMFROGLOGIC HQ

HOOYAH!!

MISSION 2 : WIDE GRIP PUSH-UPS

DOC FROG™

UPPER BODY
MISSION TWO : WIDE GRIP PUSH-UPS

Mission Objective: To build upper body strength through the completion of properly performed wide grip push-ups.

Mental Note:

Every exercise gets a little harder. If you're struggling a little bit then blast some awesome motivational music on your MP3 player. Turn it up! Loud and Proud!

Healthy ★ Food... Healthy Fuel! ★

Nutritional Schedule:

Breakfast – ✓

Egg and spinach omelet. Some organic Turkey Bacon. A glass of lemon water.

Snack 1 –

A handful of Goji berries, Blueberries and Almonds. A big glass of water.

"An apple a day."

Lunch –

A turkey Burger on a whole wheat bun. A Green Smoothie drink.

BIG glass of WATER!

ORGANIC

Snack 2 –

An Organic Apple.

Dinner –

A Chicken breast. Frozen Spinach covered in lemon juice. A big glass of water.

FFMK0001 ISSUED BY
TEAMFROGLOGIC HQ

INTRO

HOOYAH recruits, way to finish Mission 1, Push-Ups. I'm super proud of you and the effort you're making to get physically, mentally and spiritually stronger. With every mission you complete, your Froglogic™ Triad will grow stronger. Your ability to Embrace Fear, Forge your Self-Confidence™ and Live the Team Life all comes from the Love you feel for yourself and for your team. This Love will spark the fire in your gut or internal desire to take care of your body, mind and spirit. Chances are pretty high that you, just like me, have faced some Real World Challenges in your daily life or Daily Ops. These challenges might include a bully at school, troubled home life, or even a debilitating sickness or injury. Whatever negative insurgency is hammering you, you must have faith in the Love you feel for yourself as well as the Love your team feels for you. In my darkest hours I always think about this incredible gift. Love is the greatest piece of Kit or gear I've ever learned how to use. It helps me stay focused on the most positive things in my life. It helps to motivate me to grow stronger every day. And it helps me stay committed to my Team.

I try to PT every day. Especially when I'm having tough days. When I'm getting hammered by

INTRO

life, there's nothing better than knocking out a tough PT routine. It helps me clear my head and get refocused on my body, mind and spirit. Each exercise makes me stronger and enhances the Love I feel for myself. You can do this too. By PTing every day, you are learning to embrace your fears and forging your Self-Confidence. Your entire life improves, which in turn helps you be a better teammate to your family and friends. It's really that simple Recruit. You can do it.

You've started building your upper body strength with Regular Push-Ups; now let's take it up a notch and try Wide Grip Push-Ups. You are still working the same muscle groups but now you're putting a little more stress on your chest and shoulders. This exercise is a little mor difficult and requires you to push yourself a littl harder. Let the Love you have inside inspire your effort to get stronger. ✓

FFMK0001 ISSUED BY
TEAMFROGLOGIC HQ

WIDE GRIP PUSH-UPS
How to do Wide Grip Push-Ups

Step 1. With The Box™ carefully positioned on the ground, place yourself at one end of The Box™ in the Standing Ready Position. Hands down next to your sides. Feet shoulder width apart. Maintain a focused energetic attitude and believe in yourself!

Step 2. Place yourself in the modified Leaning Rest position. Knees down, feet together and toes placed on The Box™ surface. Hands placed palms down two inches wider than shoulder width apart. Keep your elbows straight.

PUSH-UPS™

THE BOX™
TEAM FROGLOGIC

Muscles Used:
Biceps. Triceps. Shoulders. Traps. Lats. Neck. Hands. Forearms. Core. Gluts. Hammys. Quads. Pectorals.

FFMK0001 ISSUED BY
TEAMFROGLOGIC HQ

WIDE GRIP PUSH-UPS

Step 3. Raise your knees off The Box, keeping your bac
straight and head up. This is the Leaning Rest, Ready
Up position.

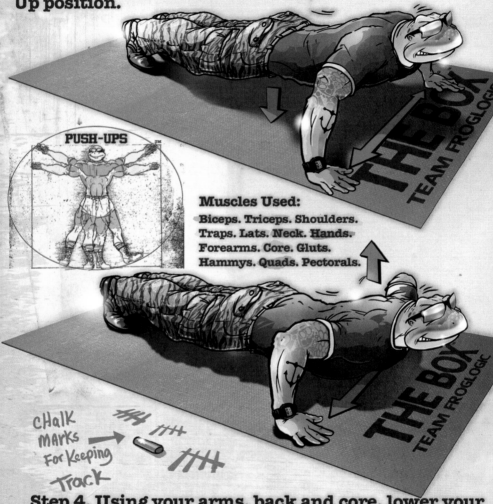

Muscles Used:
Biceps. Triceps. Shoulders.
Traps. Lats. Neck. Hands.
Forearms. Core. Gluts.
Hammys. Quads. Pectorals.

Chalk Marks For Keeping Track

Step 4. Using your arms, back and core, lower your
chest downward to The Box. Stop approximately a
fist's distance from The Box surface. Make sure to
keep your elbows tight against your sides.

FFMK0001 ISSUED BY
TEAMFROGLOGIC HQ

WIDE GRIP PUSH-UPS

Step 5. Using your arms, back and activated core, push your body back into the Ready or Up position. Fired up recruit, you just did a Push-Up!

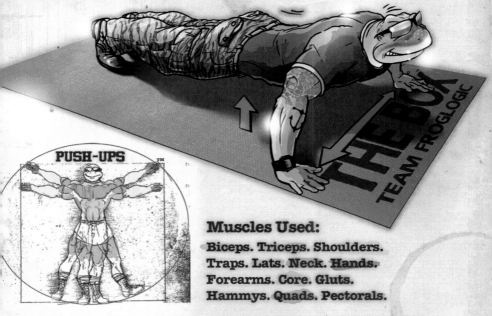

Muscles Used:
Biceps. Triceps. Shoulders.
Traps. Lats. Neck. Hands.
Forearms. Core. Gluts.
Hammys. Quads. Pectorals.

Step 6. Repeat again and again according to the amount shown in your Froglogic™ PT Schedule.

Step 7. When Counting, you should sound off with a loud and thunderous "1" after you have returned to the Leaning Rest or Ready Position. When leading a team, make sure the leader sounds off to direct the group by issuing a preparatory command of "Down" to instruct the team to move down and "Up" to get them up into the Ready Position.

WIDE GRIP PUSH-UPS

Modified Wide Grip Push-Ups:

Okay, I hear you loud and clear, <u>Wide Grips</u> <u>are harder than Regular Push-Ups</u>. That's the Point, Recruit. If you begin feeling a little hammered simply drop your knees down to The Box surface into the modified Leaning Rest Position Then drive on. Continue your PT routine and forging your body. Eventually you'll increase your strength and be able to finish all of the PT as listed.

Mental Note:

Forging your mental fortitude requires you to push past your comfort Zones and embrace the beauty of achieving real hard things in life. Remember, Life is hard so pushing yourself during PT is a great way to train your brain for life.

HOOYAH

Enhanced Wide Grip Push-Ups:

Okay Recruits, STILL feeling Froggie? If you've forged your arms, back and Core Abs into raw steel after pounding out Wide Grip Push-Ups an feel like a harder challenge, stand by for Wide Stance Wide Grip Push-Ups. Go to DocFrog.com,™ PT to see Doc Frog's™ demo instructions.

FFMK0001 ISSUED BY
TEAMFROGLOGIC HQ

Froglogic™ PT Schedule
ide Grip Push-Ups:

Reps ets	Mon	Tues	Wed	Thur	Fri
	3,4,6	4,6,8	5,5,5	10,10	MONSTER MASH
	5,4,2	6,5,4	4,4,4	7,7	MONSTER MASH
	3,4,6	5,6,3	3,3,3,3	5,5,2	MONSTER MASH

Take a 10 second break between each repetition.
Don't exceed 30 seconds between sets.

DEBRIEF:
Where do I need improvement?

cleaR my mind of "CAN'T"

_____

_____

_____

_____

_____

_____

_____

_____

_____

FFMK0001 ISSUED BY
TEAMFROGLOGIC HQ

MISSION 3 : DIAMOND PUSH-UPS

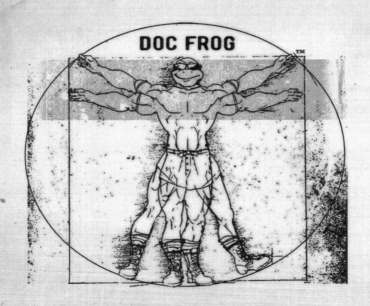

DOC FROG™

FFMK0001 ISSUED BY
TEAMFROGLOGIC HQ

UPPER BODY
MISSION THREE : DIAMOND PUSH-UPS

Mission Objective: To prepare your upper body or the ultimate outdoor adventure or activity.

Mental Note:
Diamond push-ups are killers. Take t slow and perform each one to erfection and you will see huge esults in a short period of time.

Organic
Chicken sandwich

Nutritional Schedule:

reakfast –

wo egg whites. A half grapefruit. A big glass of lemon water.

nack 1 –

handful of grapes and small handful of Goji erries. A big glass of water.

It's MY Choice... Healthy!

unch –

n organic chicken sandwich with lettuce, cucumbers, onions d tomato. On whole wheat bread. A big glass of water.

nack 2 –

andful of raw almonds and carrots.

inner –

Salmon fillet with seasoned vegetables. A glass of Almond Milk.

INTRO

Now you're on a roll, Recruit, and that get
me sooo fired up. HOOYAH! Come on, do it
with me. Let out a loud and thunderous
HOOYAH. Awesome, I know that feels
great. Just like your body feels great, too,
after doing your exercises. The more you
forge the Froglogic™ Triad, the more succes
you will have in Mission:Life. With each
exercise you complete, a little piece of you
body, mind and spirit grows stronger. The
muscle tissue in your chest and shoulders
tightens. The mental focus required to com
plete your PT helps you be more positive.
And the increased sense of pride you feel i
the Love that builds in your spirit. I feel it
for you too, knowing that you are pushing
yourself to be better. Taking action to buil
our bodies is a blessing that improves you
little bit more every time you PT.

GET SOME!

Rock on, Recruit! You're doing great, now
let's crush those triceps. Diamond Push-Up
are really really tough and should be a crit
ical piece of your upper body PT routine.
They will seem a little strange at first but

22

INTRO

tick with 'em. Just let the confidence in your earlier success help push past the awkwardness of the exercise. Many things in life can be a little awkward. It's mission critical to drive on, and work your way through unknown problems and situations. So let's knock out   those Diamond Push-Ups.

HOOYAh recruit!

DIAMOND PUSH-UPS:

How to do Diamond Push-Ups:

Step 1. With The Box™ carefully positioned on the ground, place yourself at one end of The Box™ in the Standing Ready Position. Hands down next to your sides. Feet shoulder width apart. Put a loving smile on your face and get fired up.

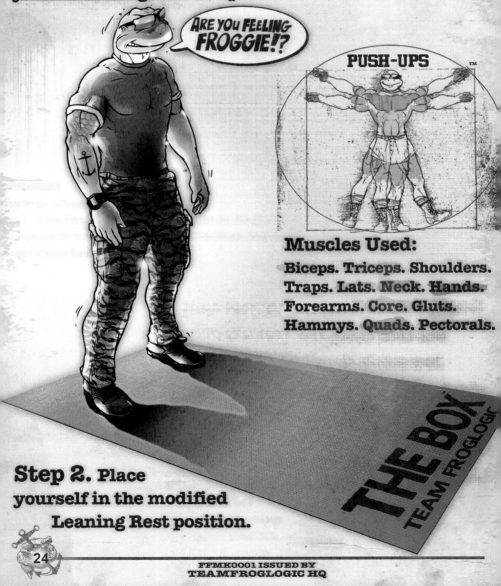

ARE YOU FEELING FROGGIE!?

PUSH-UPS ™

Muscles Used:

Biceps. Triceps. Shoulders. Traps. Lats. Neck. Hands. Forearms. Core. Gluts. Hammys. Quads. Pectorals.

Step 2. Place yourself in the modified Leaning Rest position.

THE BOX™ TEAM FROGLOGIC

FFMK0001 ISSUED BY
TEAMFROGLOGIC HQ

DIAMOND PUSH-UPS:

(Step 2 cont.) Knees down, feet together and toes placed on The Box™ surface. Hands placed palms down and touching your pointer fingers and thumbs together forming a diamond shape. Extend the rest of your fingers as far apart as possible to help with balance. Keep your elbows straight.

Muscles Used:
Biceps. Triceps. Shoulders. Traps. Lats. Neck. Hands. Forearms. Core. Gluts. Hammys. Quads. Pectorals.

Step 3. Raise your knees off The Box™ and spread your feet apart to four inches wider than shoulder width. Keep your back straight and head up. This is the Leaning Rest, Ready or Up Diamond position.

FFMK0001 ISSUED BY
TEAMFROGLOGIC HQ

DIAMOND PUSH-UPS:

Step 4. Using your arms, back and core, lower your chest downward to The Box.™ Try to touch the center part of your chest to the middle of th diamond created by your hands just above The Box™ surface. In this exercise your elbows can pivot in the opposite direction of your hand placement, facing away from your body.

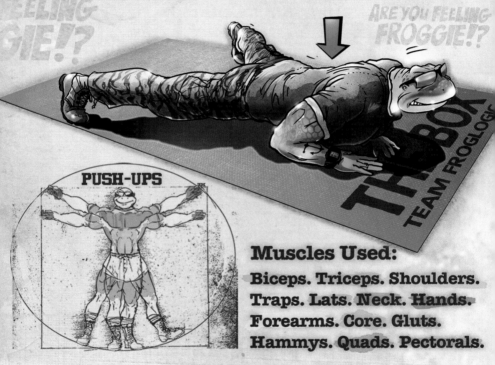

PUSH-UPS

ARE YOU FEELING FROGGIE!?

Muscles Used:
Biceps. Triceps. Shoulders. Traps. Lats. Neck. Hands. Forearms. Core. Gluts. Hammys. Quads. Pectorals.

Step 5. Using your arms, back and activated Core Abs, push your body back into the Ready or Up position. HOOYAH, you just did a Diamond Push-Up.

FFMK0001 ISSUED BY
TEAMFROGLOGIC HQ

DIAMOND PUSH-UPS:

Step 6. Repeat again and again according to the amount shown in your Froglogic™ PT Schedule.

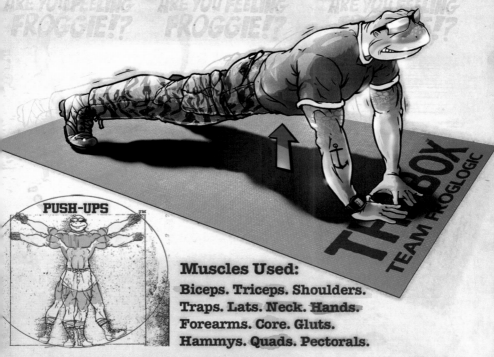

Muscles Used:
Biceps. Triceps. Shoulders. Traps. Lats. Neck. Hands. Forearms. Core. Gluts. Hammys. Quads. Pectorals.

Step 7. When Counting, you should sound off with a loud and thunderous "1" after you have returned to the Leaning Rest or Ready Position. When leading a team, make sure the leader sounds off to direct the group by issuing a preparatory command of "Down" to instruct the team to move down and "Up" to get them up into the Ready Position. With a team or swim buddy make sure everyone sounds off.

ARE YOU FEELING FROGGIE!?

Modified Push-Ups:

I know these are twice as hard as the Wide Grip Push-Ups. Suck it up. Your Triceps are going to be like forged steel. If you begin feeling a little smoked, simply drop your knees down to The Box surface into the modified Leaning Res Carry on, Recruit. Continue your PT exercises and harden that physical, mental and spiritual life.

Mental Note:

When forging your body, it's critical to think about hammerin specific muscles with specific PT exercises. The same is true in living the Team Life. We require specific detailed training for specific feelings and thoughts. Train Hard, Train Smart.

Enhanced Push-Ups:

Okay Recruits, are you feeling Froggie? The time has come and you've perfected the Diamond Push-Ups. You can perform 20 perfec Diamonds, right? Now it's time to test those Triceps with a real beating. Stand by for Dia-mond Ball Push-Ups. If you're up for the test, go to www.DocFrog.com/PT to see Doc Frog's™ demo and instructions.

Froglogic™ PT Schedule
Diamond Push-Ups:

Reps Sets	Mon	Tues	Wed	Thur	Fri
1	2,2,2	4,6,8	4,4,4	1,2,3,4,5	MONSTER MASH
3	3,3,3	5,4,3	4,4,4	5,4,3,2,1	MONSTER MASH
3	2,2,2	4,4,4	4,4,4	10	MONSTER MASH

Take a 10 second break between each repetition.
Don't exceed 30 seconds between steps.

DEBRIEF:

_____

_____

_____

_____

_____

_____

_____

_____

_____

It never gets easier...
I just get STRONGER!

BATTLE 2: CORE ABS
MISSION 4 : CRUNCHES

DOC FROG

FFMK0001 ISSUED BY
TEAMFROGLOGIC HQ

CORE ABS
MISSION FOUR: CRUNCHES

Mission Objective: To begin crushing your core abs and building your core so you can take head-on all the hard core challenges of Mission:Life.

Mental Note:
Your whole body relies on a strong core. The stronger your core is, the stronger you are physically, mentally and spiritually. Intestinal fortitude is a great piece of gear or kit for Mission:Life.

eat the BEST!!
Leave the rest!

Nutritional Schedule:

Breakfast –
A bowl of Oatmeal with Almond butter and raisins and cinnamon. Pour a glass of Almond milk on the Oatmeal.

Snack 1 –
Two organic tangerines. A glass of water.

Lunch –
Four Turkey (organic Lunch meat) and cheese roll ups. Sliced cucumbers. A big glass of water.

Snack 2 –
A hand full of grapes and cashews.

PORK CHOPS! YAY!

Dinner –
One Pork Chop. Applesauce and wild rice. A big glass of water.

FFMK0001 ISSUED BY
TEAMFROGLOGIC HQ

INTRO

Fired up, Recruits. You've just crushed the first battle in my Basic PT Manual, Battle One - Upper Body. HOOYAH. By learning how to perform these basic but very important foundations of PT, you're on your way to making sure you have all the physical requirements you'll need to lead a healthy Team Life. There is something totally empowering in being able to complete 10 perfect regular, wide grip and diamond push-ups all in a row. That's what's so awesome about conducting regular daily PT. You feel more Self-Confiden and ready to embrace the nasty little fear that seem to pop up in Mission:Life when your body isn't as strong as you would lik it to be. With every challenge we face hea on in life, we get stronger. Easy Day.

Okay Operator, now for your next Battle: CORE ABS. Time to light the fire in your gut because this battle is going to require a whole new level of hard work coming from you and your swim buddy. Think about how many times a day you use your Core Abdominal muscles.

FFMK0001 ISSUED BY
TEAMFROGLOGIC HQ

INTRO

The answer is a **METRIC TON!** Everything we do requires us to contract our Core Abs at some point. Getting out of bed in the morning. Taking a shower. Eating. NOW, think about all the active stuff you love doing every day. Skateboarding, Surfing, Snowboarding, Mountain Biking, Soccer, Football, Softball, Cheerleading; all demand high levels of Core Abs strength in order to excel in these awesome sports. Not only do our Core Abs help with the very important balance aspects of physical activity, but also having strong Core Abs allows you to maintain your Breathing Composure or Wind during vigorous activity. Developing the muscles in your stomach helps every aspect of living a healthy lifestyle including balance, posture, speed, endurance, strength and intestinal fortitude.

Recruit, I've been training for most of my life. One huge lesson learned from all my years of training, both as a Navy Frogman and as Lead Instructor for Team Froglogic, is that strong Core Abs equal a strong personal resolve or intestinal fortitude.

FFMK0001 ISSUED BY
TEAMFROGLOGIC HQ

INTRO

It works like this: forging your Core Abs is hard work and takes a focused determination that keeps you going when you don't feel like doing another Crunch, Knee Up Outer Oblique, or 4 Count Flutter Kick. When the discomfort in your stomach is screaming in your ear to STOP, you ignore the whining and drive on. That voice screaming in your head is coming from your worst enemy, Old Mr. Murphy. Old Mr. Murphy is the voice of your fears, your lack of self-confidence and your misguided desire to go through life on your own. You see Recruit, life is hard and while you're conducting your Mission:Life, Old Mr. Murphy is going to try to get you to quit by seeding just a small dose of negativity in your head. Each time you do another repetition of any one of my exercises in this or any other manual, you're taking control of your life and quieting the negative insurgency Old Mr. Murphy is constantly wagin against you. The more you do this in your physical PT, the easier it becomes when you're conducting mental and spiritual PT as well. Forge your Core Abs day in and da

34

INTRO

ut by making sure you and your team are
onstantly telling Old Mr. Murphy to keep
t Locked Up!

Crunches:

How to do a Crunch:

tep 1. With The Box™ carefully positioned
n the ground, place yourself in the middle
f The Box™. Now lie down on your back.

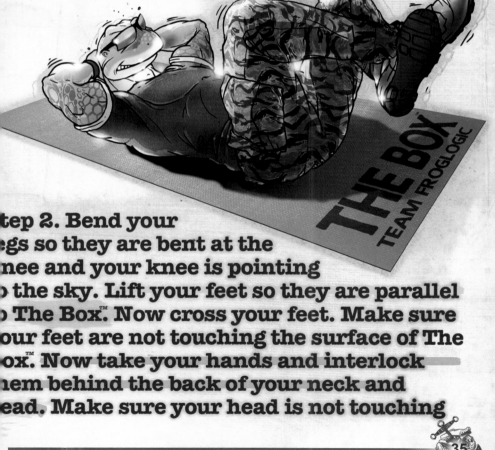

THE BOX
TEAM FROGLOGIC

tep 2. Bend your
egs so they are bent at the
nee and your knee is pointing
 the sky. Lift your feet so they are parallel
 The Box™. Now cross your feet. Make sure
our feet are not touching the surface of The
ox™. Now take your hands and interlock
em behind the back of your neck and
ead. Make sure your head is not touching

CRUNCHES

(Step 2 cont.) the surface of The Box.™ This is your Ready Position for Crunches.

Step 3. Contract your Core Abs and move your elbows forward and up towards your knees, attempting to touch your knees with your elbows. Once you have crunched your upper body and lower body together, try to hold the position for at least half a second. This is the Up Position for Crunches.

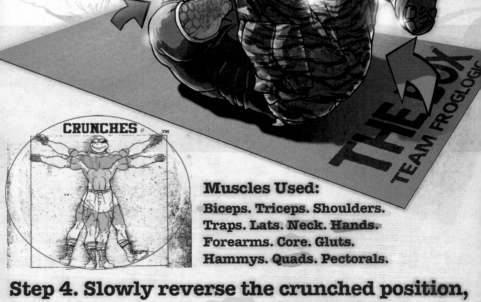

CRUNCHES ™

Muscles Used:
Biceps. Triceps. Shoulders. Traps. Lats. Neck. Hands. Forearms. Core. Gluts. Hammys. Quads. Pectorals.

Step 4. Slowly reverse the crunched position, returning to the Ready Position with your back flat on The Box.™

FFMK0001 ISSUED BY
TEAMFROGLOGIC HQ

CRUNCHES

Step 5. Repeat over and over again. Make sure your head and feet DO NOT touch the surface of your PT platform until you have completed all the required number of repetitions.

THE BOX
TEAM FROGLOGIC

CRUNCHES ™

Muscles Used:
**Biceps. Triceps. Shoulders.
Traps. Lats. Neck. Hands.
Forearms. Core. Gluts.
Hammys. Quads. Pectorals.**

Step 6. When Counting, you should sound off with a loud and thunderous "1" after you have returned to the Down or Ready Position. When leading a team, make sure the leader sounds off to direct the group by issuing a preparatory command of "Up" to instruct the team to move up and "Down" to get them to the Ready Position. Then everyone should sound off by saying "1!"

FFMK0001 ISSUED BY
TEAMFROGLOGIC HQ

Modified Crunches:

If you begin feeling a little hammered, simply drop your knees and feet down to The Box™ surface into the modified Crunch Position. Instead of rolling your elbows all the way up to your knees, keep your hands interlocked behind your head and roll your shoulders off the deck just a few inches. It is important that you hold the Up Position for at least one second. Then drive on. Continue your PT routine and forging your body. Eventually you'll increase your strength and be able to finish all of the PT as listed.

Mental Note:

Everything you do in life requires a strong physical core or intestinal fortitude. This means that you need a strong gut to endure the challenges of Mission: Life.

Go Big!

Enhanced Crunches: HOOYAH!!

HOOYAH Recruit, I think you're ready to test your Core. Well, are you? Every time you perform a proper Crunch, try to hold the Up Position for at least five seconds. The burn you feel in your Core Abs will pay huge rewards in helping you have what it takes to support your frame and excel at sports and outdoor extreme activities.

FFMK0001 ISSUED BY
TEAMFROGLOGIC HQ

roglogic™ PT Schedule
runches:

Reps sets	Mon	Tues	Wed	Thur	Fri
	10,10	15,15	5,5,5,5	10,20	
	10,5	10,15	7,7,7,7	20,10	MONSTER MASH
	2,4,6	2,4,6,4,2	5,5,3,3	20,10,15	MONSTER MASH

Take a 10 second break between each repetition.
Don't exceed 30 seconds between sets.

DEBRIEF:

PRACTICE to Perfection!

_____

_____

_____

_____

_____

_____

_____

_____

_____

_____

_____

_____

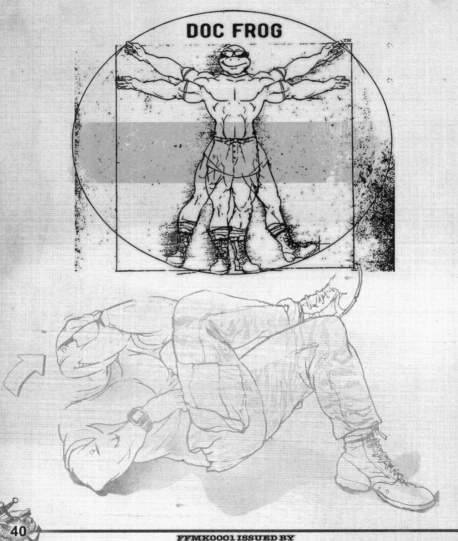

MISSION 5 : KNEE UP OUTER OBLIQUES

DOC FROG

FFMK0001 ISSUED BY
TEAMFROGLOGIC HQ

CORE ABS
MISSION FIVE : OUTER OBLIQUE CRUNCHES

Mission Objective: To isolate specific core abdominal muscles by using specific body positions. ✓

Mental Note:

Isolating specific parts of our body, mind and spirit is necessary in order to get a comprehensive workout. Remember, it's critical to have balance in Mission: Life.

PB&J!! ⬇

Nutritional Schedule:

Breakfast –

Plain non-fat Greek Yogurt. Granola or Cereal of choice. Mix the two. A big glass of lemon water.

Snack 1 –

An Organic Apple. A big glass of water.

Lunch –

PB&J with ground peanut butter, organic jelly on 12-grain bread. A big glass of water.

Snack 2 –

A bowl full of walnuts and Goji berries.

Dinner –

Spaghetti with an organic Turkey based meat sauce. A big glass of water.

FFMK0001 ISSUED BY
TEAMFROGLOGIC HQ

INTRO

AWESOME RECRUIT! Well done. Way to crus
yourself on Mission 4. I'm super stoked. The
last few were killers, huh? No rest for the
weary. Let's get back at it. Doing Crunches
meant you were Hammering the middle part
of your stomach muscles, the largest part of
your Core Ab muscle group. Now let's move to
your outer little muscles in your Core Abs. You
Outer Obliques play a major role in your physical stabilization or balance and really help wi
all types of twisting and swinging movements
These little suckers are hard to hit so we need
isolate them in a more focused fashion. Just be
cause they're small doesn't mean you can blow
these smaller muscles off. Let's get started wit
Knee Up Outer Oblique Crunches. The cool thin
about this exercise is that by adjusting anothe
body part, you can really isolate and focus on
the muscles you want to crush. Another cool
thing is that you're working your main Core
Abs too. Remember that the body functions as
a total unit. You need to be considerate of all
the smaller muscle groups, which will ultimat
ly help your big muscles perform better.

Life is a lot like working those smaller muscle
groups. It's critical to pay attention to the littl
things you do every day to make a difference i

42

INTRO

your overall **Big Missions in life.** The little Ops and actions you perform which make up a big chunk of your day need to be completed with precision and focus. If these actions seem to have little or no meaning to you or your team, that's **UNSAT.** Think about it, Recruit! If you don't pay attention to the details, you're going to miss all the little critical pieces of Intel and tactical applications that help you succeed as a Team Froglogic™ Operator. It's the little details that matter most in Mission:Life.

WHew!--
....but
AWesome!

FFMK0001 ISSUED BY
TEAMFROGLOGIC HQ

KNEE UP OUTER OBLIQUE CRUNCHES:

How to do a Knee Up Outer Oblique Crunch

Step 1. With The Box™ carefully positioned on the ground, place yourself in the middle of the PT Platform. Now lie down on your back.

Step 2. Bend your knees in Sit-Up flexed position. Make sure your feet are flat on the surface of The Box.™

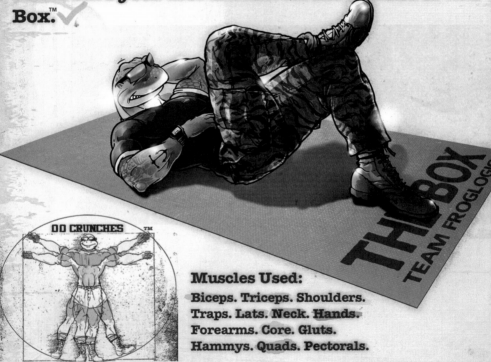

Muscles Used:
Biceps. Triceps. Shoulders. Traps. Lats. Neck. Hands. Forearms. Core. Gluts. Hammys. Quads. Pectorals.

Step 3. Lift up your right foot, place it on top of your left knee and rest it in place. Take your left hand and grab the back part of the base of your head. Make sure to keep your head off the surface of The Box™ with your elbow pointed away from your ear.

FFMK0001 ISSUED BY
TEAMFROGLOGIC HQ

KNEE UP OUTER OBLIQUE CRUNCHES:

(Step 3 cont.) Place your right hand, palm down on your belly button. This is the Ready Position for Knee Up Outer Oblique Crunches.

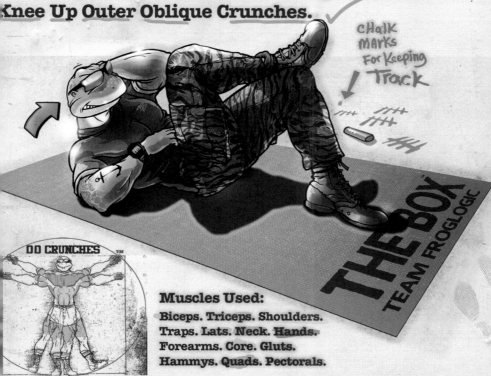

Chalk Marks For Keeping Track

DO CRUNCHES ™

Muscles Used:
Biceps. Triceps. Shoulders. Traps. Lats. Neck. Hands. Forearms. Core. Gluts. Hammys. Quads. Pectorals.

Step 4. Contract your Core Abs, raise your left elbow up and attempt to touch your right knee with the tip of your elbow. Make sure to hold your elbow to knee for at least a half second. This is the Up Position.

Step 5. Slightly release your Core Ab contraction and return to the Ready Position.

FFMK0001 ISSUED BY
TEAMFROGLOGIC HQ

KNEE UP OUTER OBLIQUE CRUNCHES:

(Step 5 cont.) This is the return to the Ready Position.

Step 6. <u>Repeat over and over again.</u> Make sure your head DOES NOT touch the surface of your PT Platform until you have completed all the required number repetitions.

Step 7. When finished with the suggested number of repetitions, switch your right

FFMK0001 ISSUED BY
TEAMFROGLOGIC HQ

KNEE UP OUTER OBLIQUE CRUNCHES:

(Step 7 cont.) foot to the down position and raise your left foot to your right knee. Remove your left hand from behind your head and place it on your stomach. Place your right hand behind your head, putting your body in the Ready Position to begin Knee Up Outer Ab   Crunches for the other side of your   Core Abs.

Muscles Used:
Biceps. Triceps. Shoulders. Traps. Lats. Neck. Hands. Forearms. Core. Gluts. Hammys. Quads. Pectorals.

Step 8. Repeat over and over again. Make sure your head **DOES NOT** touch the surface of your PT Platform until you have completed all the required number of repetitions.

FFMK0001 ISSUED BY
TEAMFROGLOGIC HQ

KNEE UP OUTER OBLIQUE CRUNCHES
Modified Crunches:

If you begin feeling a little hammered, simply drop your foot down to The Box™ surface into the Modified Outer Ab Crunch Position. Instead of rolling your elbow all the way up to your knee, keep your hand behind your head and roll your shoulder off the deck just a few inches. Try to move your elbow in the same manner as if your knee was still up. It's important that you hold the Up Position for at least one second. Then drive on. Continue your PT routine and forging your body. Eventually you'll increase your strength and be able to finish all of the PT as listed.

Mental Note:
When you get into tough situations in life, you sometimes feel like your guts are turning inside out. That's why it's important to work on your physical, mental and spiritual core all the time.

Enhanced Knee Up Outer Oblique Ab Crunches

Is it Froggie time? Let's see how strong you're getting. Every time you perform a proper Knee Up Outer Ab Crunch, try to hold the Up Position for at least five seconds. The burn you feel in your Outer Core Abs will pay huge rewards in helping you excel at sports and outdoor extreme activities. Crush your Crunch!

FFMK0001 ISSUED BY
TEAMFROGLOGIC HQ

roglogic™ PT Schedule
nee Up Outer Oblique Ab Crunches:

Reps Sets	Mon	Tues	Wed	Thur	Fri
	Lt 5,5 Rt 5,5	Lt 10 Rt 10	Lt 5 Rt 5	Lt 20 Rt 20	MONSTER MASH
	Lt 4,4 Rt 4,4	Lt 5 Rt 5	Lt 20 Rt 20	Lt 10 Rt 10	MONSTER MASH
	Lt 3,3 Rt 3,3	Lt 3 Rt 3	Lt 5 Rt 5	Lt 10 Rt 10	MONSTER MASH

Take a 10 second break between each repetition.
Don't exceed 30 seconds between sets.

DEBRIEF: ✓

Commit
2 Be
★ Fit!!

_____

_____

_____

_____

_____

_____

_____

_____

_____

_____

_____

_____

MISSION 6 : FLUTTER KICKS

DOC FROG

FFMK0001 ISSUED BY
TEAMFROGLOGIC HQ

CORE ABS
MISSION SIX: FLUTTER KICKS

Mission Objective: To crush yourself with one of the greatest frogman exercises of all time.

Mental Note:
Okay Recruit, here we go with your favorite exercise and mine, 4 Count Flutter Kicks. As your hip flexors begin to burn, think about all those who've come before you strengthening their bodies by doing thousands of these nasty little crushers. Be proud that you're part of that group now. HOOYAH!!

Nutritional Schedule:

Breakfast -
French toast with organic eggs. Honey drizzle and blueberries. A glass of almond milk. ✓

Snack 1 -
Banana. A big glass of water.

Lunch -
Grilled Cheese and 12-grain bread. Small bowl of Tomato Soup. A big glass of water.

Snack 2 -
Naturally ground almond butter on apple slices. A big glass of water.

Dinner -
Meatloaf and spinach with garlic and lemon. A big glass of water. H2O!!

FFMK0001 ISSUED BY
TEAMFROGLOGIC HQ

INTRO
4 COUNT FLUTTER KICKS,
"Your Favorite and Mine"

4 Count Flutter Kicks, your favorite and MINE
I Love Flutter Kicks, Recruit. Every self-respecting frogman loves doing Flutter Kicks until the cows come home. Flutter Kicks help Operators with our ruck (backpack), running, swimming and airborne operations. Flutter Kicks will help you with baseball, volleyball, snowboarding, motocross, track and of course, swimming. I've done millions of these amazing exercises in my life and you should too.

The awesome thing about Flutter Kicks is the awesome way your Core Abs, Hip Flexors and upper legs all work together to give you a sick workout. Now, here's the deal: when you do enough of these you're going to get hammered, period. It is what it is. However, the strength you gain not only physically but also mentally and spiritually is massive. As you shout out your own cadence or count for your team while doing these 4 count crushers you're gonna be humbled. That's the point. When you're gasping for air on number 20 and it feels like your guts are flipping inside out, just think to yourself, "I can do this, I will never quit." Then straighten your back,

FFMK0001 ISSUED BY
TEAMFROGLOGIC HQ

INTRO

uck your chin a little tighter to your chest and
ound off with a loud and thunderous "20!"
Remember recruits, your favorite and mine.
eady, Begin. OOUUTT

ow to do a 4 Count Flutter Kick:

tep 1. With The Box™ carefully positioned on the
round, place yourself in the middle of The Box.™
ow lie down on your back.

tep 2. Slide your hands under your body. Place
our knuckles flat on The Box™ surface and then
osition

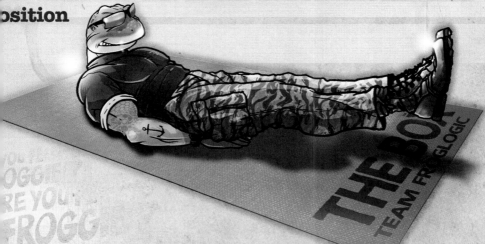

em just underneath the outside edge of your
utt. This will give your lower back support dur-
g this exercise. Lift your head off The Box™ so
our chin is almost touching your chest and hold
there. Raise your legs 12 inches off The Box™
urface keeping your feet together, toes pointing

(Step 2 cont.) to the sky. This is the Ready Position for doing your favorite exercise and mine.

Step 3. Begin the exercise by performing a scissor kick leading with your left foot moving from 12 inches to 18 inches off The Box™ surface. At the same time move your right

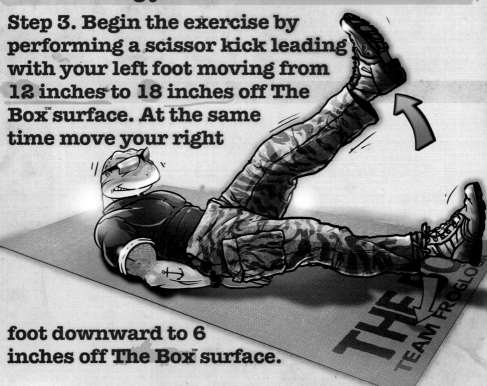

foot downward to 6 inches off The Box™ surface.

Step 4. Reverse the scissor kick, moving your right foot to the top position (18 inches) and your left foot to the lower position (6 inches).

Step 5. When counting during this exercise you will use a 4 Count counting system. This means as you begin the exercise by lifting your left foot to the up position, sound off by saying the number "1" out loud.

FFMK0001 ISSUED BY
TEAMFROGLOGIC HQ

(Step 5 cont.) As you reverse your feet by executing the required scissor kick and your right foot is in the up position sound off by saying the number "2" out loud. Reverse again and say the number "3." The four count is finished when you

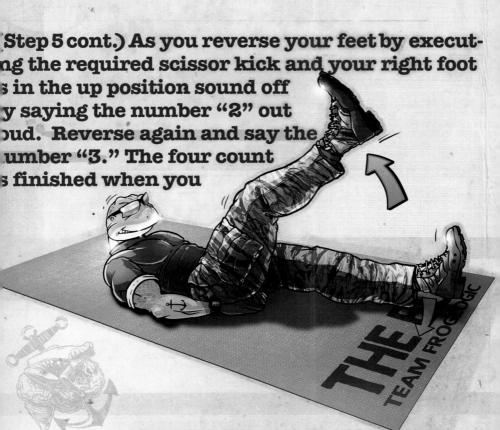

reverse your feet for the last time in this repetition and sound off by saying the number of the repetition. Example, "1,2,3,1. 1,2,3,2. 1,2,3,3. 1,2,3,4. 1,2,3,5." Easy Day.

FLUTTER KICKS ™

Muscles Used:

Biceps. Triceps. Shoulders.
Traps. Lats. Neck. Hands.
Forearms. Core. Gluts.
Hammys. Quads. Pectorals.

Modified 4 Counts:

Remove your hands from the supported position. Place a folded towel beneath your butt to increase support. Place your hands palm down about 45° away from your body to increase support. This should help you perform the exercise more efficiently.

Mental Note:
The harder you work on forging your Core Abs, the stronger your spine and frame will become. Great posture and a strong gut are the perfect way to support your growing ability to embrace your fear, forge your Self-Confidence and live the Team Life.

Enhanced 4 Count Flutter Kicks:

YOU ARE CRUSHING IT NOW, RECRUIT! Bravo Zulu. Are you ready to push it just a little bit more? Then go to DocFrog.com/PT and check out instructions for Enhanced 4 Count Flutter Kicks.

HOOYAH!

NOthing WORth having comes EASY!!

Froglogic™ PT Schedule
Count Flutter Kicks:

Reps Sets	Mon	Tues	Wed	Thur	Fri
	5	10	10	20	MONSTER MASH
	10	10	15	10	MONSTER MASH
	5	10	10	20	MONSTER MASH

Take a 10 second break between each repetition.
Don't exceed 30 seconds between sets.

DEBRIEF:

THe best way to predict my future is to CREATE it!

_____

_____

_____

_____

_____

_____

_____

_____

_____

_____

_____

_____

BATTLE 3 : LOWER BODY
MISSION 7 : AIR SQUATS

DOC FROG

FFMK0001 ISSUED BY
TEAMFROGLOGIC HQ

LOWER BODY
MISSION SEVEN: AIR SQUATS

Mission Objective: Time to strengthen your foundation. Crush your lower body leg exercises and prepare yourself for the race of life.

Mental Note:

Think about how many thousands of miles your legs will carry you in life. Now think about how many hundreds of thousands of awesome adventures you'll have outdoors if your lower body is like steel. Time to forge your legs. HOOYAH!!

Nutritional Schedule:

Breakfast –
Two hard boiled eggs. A banana. A big glass of lemon water.

Snack 1 –
Three slices of watermelon. A box of raisins. A big glass of water.

California Raisins!

Lunch –
A ham and cheese sandwich.
A glass of Almond milk.

Snack 2 –
A handful of raw walnuts. Some dates. A big glass of water.

Dinner –
A meatloaf dinner. Steamed green beans covered in lemons.
A big glass of water.

INTRO

HOOYAH Recruit. You're half way through my Basic PT manual. I am proud of you. You should be feeling incredibly proud for embracing the hammer and crushing yourself. You've just won two battles by pushing past the pain and fear of failure to properly complete all the Missions in the Upper Body PT battle and all the missions in the Core Abs PT battle. I bet you're feeling a lot of love for yourself! You should be. In life, we go through many tough times because life can be really hard. That's what is so awesome about being alive. Facing the challenges of your body, mind and spirit show that you're learning how to overcome your limits using the greatest tactical weapon you have to grow stronger, Love. The awesome thing about pushing yourself to embrace your fears, forge your self-confidence and live the Team Life is that every day you are gaining ground in learning to love yourself more. This is a huge part of living a healthy Froglogic™ Lifestyle. By working hard to get physically, mentally and spiritually fit, the love you feel for yourself hardens like steel. This enables you to share the strength of your love with those who matter most in your life, your TEAM.

FFMK0001 ISSUED BY
TEAMFROGLOGIC HQ

INTRO

Let's get back to training. Your next battle will help you build the strongest muscle group in your body, your legs. Every great operator at Team Froglogic™ spends tons of time forging our lower bodies in order to carry us through all of our great adventures. Mountain Climbing, Cross-Country Skiing, Paddle Boarding, Wake Surfing and Gymnastics. Without the fortified foundation of strong legs, you're gonna struggle with all physical activity. Air Squats are a great place to start. Your Quads, Hammys, Flexors, Gluts, Core Abs and lower back all play a pivotal role in your body's ability to move. And when you want to move with a purpose, these muscles, when properly conditioned, can help you become explosive. Begin to build your solid foundation with tons and tons of Air Squats. Get 'er done!

How to do an Air Squat:

Step 1. With The Box™ carefully positioned on the ground, place yourself in the middle of The Box™ with your feet shoulder width apart, arms extended straight out in front of you with your palms down. This is the Ready Position.

AIR SQUATS™

Muscles Used:
Biceps. Triceps. Shoulders.
Traps. Lats. Neck. Hands.
Forearms. Core. Gluts.
Hammys. Quads. Pectorals.

ARE YOU FEELIN FROGGIE!

THE BOX
TEAM FROGLOGIC

FFMK0001 ISSUED BY
TEAMFROGLOGIC HQ

How to do an Air Squat:

Step 2. First, engage your **Core Abs** and begin dropping your butt downward. As you bend at the waist and knees make sure to keep your spine straight, head up and knees firmly positioned over your feet. Make sure to keep the weight of your body mostly on the heels of your feet.

AIR SQUATS

THE BOX
TEAM FROGLOGIC

Muscles Used:
Biceps. Triceps. Shoulders.
Traps. Lats. Neck. Hands.
Forearms. Core. Gluts.
Hammys. Quads. Pectorals.

The **Down Position** should be when the upper part of your legs are at a greater than 90° angle. Don't lean too far forward or backward.

FFMK0001 ISSUED BY
TEAMFROGLOGIC HQ

How to do an Air Squat:

Step 3. Engage your Core Abs and begin moving back up into the Ready Position. You should feel the burn in your Gluts, Quads and Hammys. Be sure to maintain your balance by keeping your Core Abs tight and back straight. Stay off your toes and keep your head up.

AIR SQUATS ™

Muscles Used:
Biceps. Triceps. Shoulders. Traps. Lats. Neck. Hands. Forearms. Core. Gluts. Hammys. Quads. Pectorals.

Step 4. Repeat over and over again. Do as many as the PT Routine requires.

ARE YOU FEELIN FROGGIE!

THE BOX
TEAM FROGLOGIC

FFMK0001 ISSUED BY
TEAMFROGLOGIC HQ

Step 5. When Counting make sure to sound off by saying the number "1" after completing the full cycle of the exercise. When leading a team of Recruits, make sure to give the preparatory commands of "Down" and "Up" in order to make sure everyone is on the same sheet of music.

Modified Air Squats:

If you're having trouble performing the exercise effectively, place a chair behind you. When you squat down into the Down Position, allow your butt to come to rest on the front edge of the chair. Make sure your butt hits the chair. If you need to modify the exercise even more, spread your feet wider than your shoulders by two inches on either side. This should help you get the hang of the exercise and help get your balance squared away too.

Mental Note:

Your legs are the most powerful part of your body. If you dedicate yourself to strengthening your lower body then you will have the ability to carry yourself and your team farther than you could ever imagine.

Enhanced Air Squat:

Fired up Recruit, you are making the Team better with each successfully completed repetition. Thank you. Stand by to take it to the next level. Go to DocFrog.com/PT and check out the instructions on Enhanced Air Squat.

Froglogic™ PT Schedule
Air Squats:

Reps Sets	Mon	Tues	Wed	Thur	Fri
1	10	25	10	10,10	MONSTER MASH
2	10	15	30	20,20	MONSTER MASH
3	7	5	10	10,5	MONSTER MASH

Take a 10 second break between each repetition.
Don't exceed 30 seconds between sets.

DEBRIEF:

_____

_____

_____

_____

_____

66

MISSION 8 : CALF RAISES

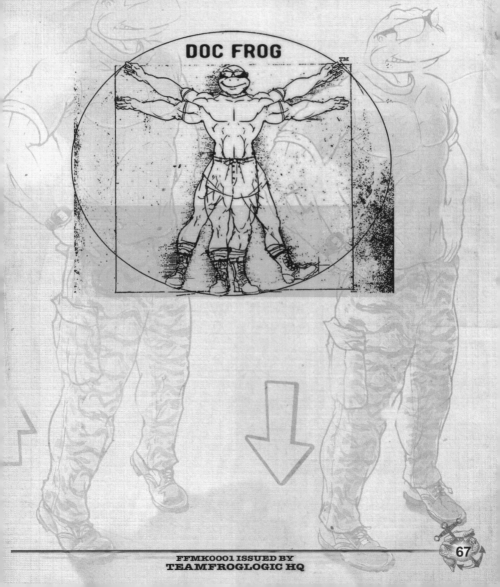

DOC FROG

LOWER BODY
MISSION EIGHT: CALF RAISES

Mission Objective: To turn your calfs and lower leg muscles into powerful pieces of gear. These muscles help you gain explosive speed and strength.

Mental Note:

There are lots of smaller exercises, mental tasks and spiritual challenges you'll face in your operational lives. Sometimes these smaller quests don't get enough of our attention. It's important to remember that even the small things require your focused attention if you want to become successful in Mission: Life.

Nutritional Schedule:

Breakfast –
A bowl of oatmeal. A half grapefruit.
A glass of lemon water.

Snack 1 –
A handful of Chocolate Goji berries
A big glass of water.

Lunch –
An Almond butter and organic jelly sandwich
with Banana slices in it. A big glass of orange
juice.

Snack 2 –
An orange.

Dinner –
A piece of line caught grouper. Some steamed organic vegetables.
A big glass of water.

Commit
to be
Fit!!

FFMK0001 ISSUED BY
TEAMFROGLOGIC HQ

INTRO

WEEEET! I'll bet your legs are on fire! Bravo Zulu, teammate. Air Squats are no joke. You're on a roll so let's keep the hammer down and move right into our next exercise, Calf Raises. Once again you need to focus on a smaller muscle group that plays a huge role in stability, agility, speed and balance. Your Calf muscles play a major role in all physical operations. Ops like Dancing, Hockey, Long Distance Running, Figure Skating and Skim Boarding. By isolating this muscle you will be able to focus on building real strength, stamina and endurance. These three things are huge in forging your Froglogic™ Triad, the body, mind and spirit.

Fear, lack of Self-Confidence and no team can cause huge problems in our lives. That's why it's mission critical to make sure you're laser focused on building strength, stamina and endurance within your body, mind and soul. Remember, life is like a long Ruck March! Experiencing life to its fullest and understanding the right lessons learned takes time. The more you prepare for this path, the better you and your team are going to be down the road. Listen up recruit, instant gratification like a Google search isn't the reality of actual living.

INTRO

You need to be patient and push yourself to proerly and slowly build your foundation. When th battle does get tough you **WILL** be victorious.

FFMK0001 ISSUED BY
TEAMFROGLOGIC HQ

ow to do Calf Raises:

tep 1. With The Box™ carefully positioned on the round, place yourself in the middle of the PT Platorm with your feet shoulder width apart and your ands placed firmly on your hips. Now slightly turn our toes inward by about an inch. This is the Ready osition.

Muscles Used:

Calfs, Gluts, Lower Legs, Core Abs

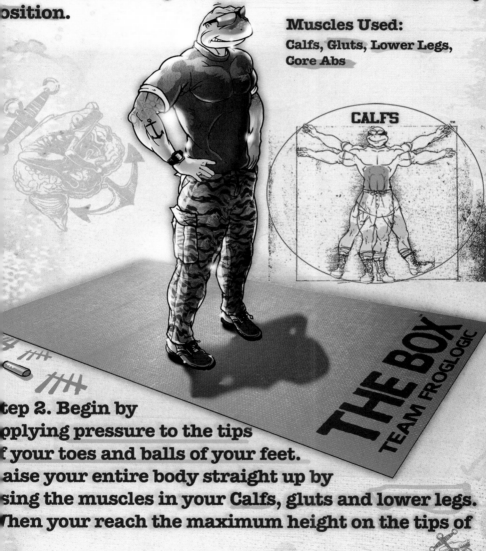

CALFS

THE BOX™
TEAM FROGLOGIC

tep 2. Begin by pplying pressure to the tips f your toes and balls of your feet. aise your entire body straight up by sing the muscles in your Calfs, gluts and lower legs. hen your reach the maximum height on the tips of

FFMK0001 ISSUED BY
TEAMFROGLOGIC HQ

(Step 2 cont.) your toes try to hold this position for a least one second. **This is the Up position.**

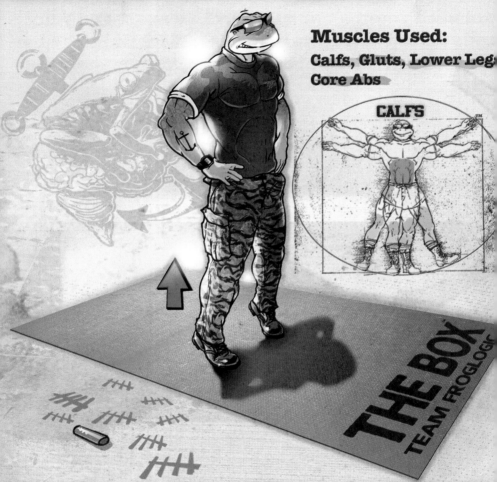

Muscles Used:
Calfs, Gluts, Lower Leg
Core Abs

CALFS

THE BOX
TEAM FROGLOGIC

Step 3. Concentrate your mind on your calf muscles as you stand as tall as possible. Return to the Ready position. This completes one cycle of the exercise.

FFMK0001 ISSUED BY
TEAMFROGLOGIC HQ

tep 4. **Repeat over and over again. Do as many as he PT Routine requires.**

tep 5. **When Counting make sure to sound off by aying the number "1" after completing the full ycle of the exercise. When leading a team of ecruits make sure to give the preparatory com- ands of Ready and Up to ensure that everyone is n the same sheet of music.**

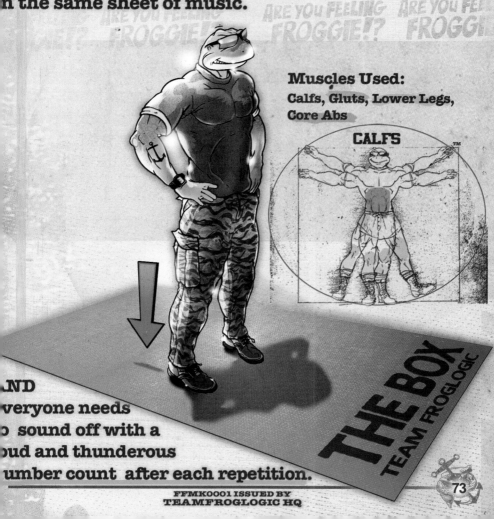

Muscles Used:
Calfs, Gluts, Lower Legs, Core Abs

CALFS

ND veryone needs sound off with a ud and thunderous umber count after each repetition.

THE BOX
TEAM FROGLOGIC

FFMK0001 ISSUED BY
TEAMFROGLOGIC HQ

Modified Calf Raises:

If you are having trouble or your calf muscles are burning out too quickly then reduce the time you hold the Up position. You can also straighten out your toes. This will help decrease the difficulty.

Mental Note:

Improving your calf muscles will increase your explosive "take off" speed. It will also increase your vertical jumping ability. Sometimes the simplest exercises can have the greatest impact on improving your physical, mental and spiritual capabilities. ✓

Enhanced Calf Raises:

Nice job. Way to get your lower body dialed in, Recruit. Thanks for putting out! If you want to build those calfs even more then go to DocFrog.co /PT to find out how. Crush it! HOOYAH

Froglogic™ PT Schedule
Calf Raises:

Reps Sets	Mon	Tues	Wed	Thur	Fri
1	10	25	10	10,10	MONSTER MASH
2	10	15	30	20,20	MONSTER MASH
3	7	5	10	10,5	MONSTER MASH

Take a 10 second break between each repetition. Don't exceed 30 seconds between sets.

DEBRIEF:

MISSION 9 : LUNGES

DOC FROG

FFMK0001 ISSUED BY
TEAMFROGLOGIC HQ

LOWER BODY
MISSION NINE = LUNGES

Mission Objective: To push yourself and your egs to the next level of Hard.

Mental Note:
Don't ever be afraid to lunge forward, taking that big leap of faith. Taking risk will enable you to embrace your fears, forge your self-onfidence and live the Team Life.

Nutritional Schedule:

Breakfast –
Two over easy eggs. Three slices of Avocado. A big glass of water with lemons.

Snack 1 –
Two tangerines. A handful of raw walnuts. A big glass of water.

Lunch –
A turkey sandwich on 12-grain bread. Some raw vegetables. A big glass of almond milk. Two tangerines. A handful of raw walnuts. A big glass of water.

Snack 2 –
Cheese and Apple slices. A big glass of Almond Milk.

Dinner –
An organic chicken breast. Frozen Spinach with garlic. Watermelon. A big glass of water.

INTRO

BURN BABY BURN! Great job on Calf Raises. Didn't think those would burn as badly as they did, huh? Stand by Recruit, it's time to put the finishing touches on those legs. Lunges are going to burn like crazy too. But you can do it. Have faith in yourself. Lunges are great lower body builders because they hammer the snot out of your Quads, Hammys, Gluts, Core Abs and Calfs. Properly performing Lunges will help you accelerate your skill sets in Diving, Wrestling, Karate, Field Hockey and Lacrosse. Heads up Recruit, this is your last exercise in this battle. So it's time to dig deep and allow yourself to lunge forward that extra bit to finish strong.

It's during these moments in your PT or in Mission:Life when that extra effort means the difference between success and failure. Now don't get me wrong, failure is a great learning tool. It teaches you what not to do and how to persevere. When you've given it your all and you've got nothing left physically, mentally and spiritually, you're good to go. However, when failure comes as a result of you quitting or not pushing yourself then you're in big time trouble. Maybe not in the exact moment, because relief has gotten the betterment of your judgment, but definitely in the long run you'll feel bad about

FFMK0001 ISSUED BY
TEAMFROGLOGIC HQ

INTRO

not following through to the end. Remember this Recruit, even though I'm your swim buddy, there is only so much I can do to motivate you.

When you're sweating bullets, your brain is burned out and your spirit feels like its gonna snap, THAT'S when you dig deep, push yourself that extra inch and finish like the true Team Froglogic™ Operator you are. HOOYAH!

LUNGES:

How to do a Lunge.

Step 1. With The Box™ carefully positioned on the ground, place yourself at the back of The Box™ with your feet shoulder width apart and your hands placed firmly on your hips. This is the Ready or Up Position.

LUNGES™

Muscles Used:
Core Abs, Hip Flexors, Quads, Gluts, Calfs, Lower Back, Shoulders

ARE YOU FEELING FROGGIE!?
ARE YOU FEELING FROGGIE!?
ARE YOU FEELING FROGGIE!?
ARE YOU FEELING FROGGIE!?

THE BOX
TEAM FROGLOGIC

Step 2. To begin the exercise step forward with your left foot, moving it just enough distance to create a 90°

FFMK0001 ISSUED BY
TEAMFROGLOGIC HQ

LUNGES:

(Step 2 cont.) angle from your knee to your back right toe. This is the Down Position.

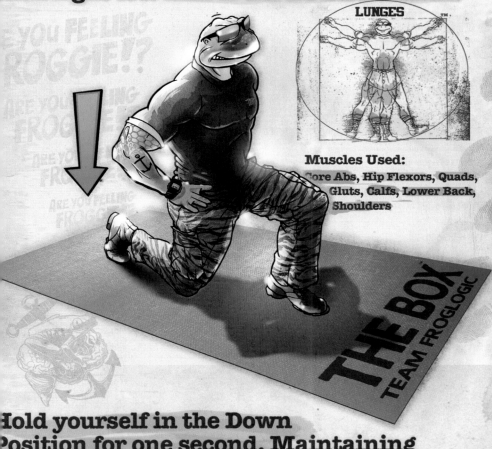

Muscles Used:
Core Abs, Hip Flexors, Quads, Gluts, Calfs, Lower Back, Shoulders

Hold yourself in the Down Position for one second. Maintaining proper form is key to getting great results. Good form also helps prevent injuries. Doing exercises properly also promotes discipline. Keep up the attention to detail. Believe me, the payoff will be HUGE!

FFMK0001 ISSUED BY
TEAMFROGLOGIC HQ

LUNGES:

Step 3. Move back to the Ready or Up position

Muscles Used:
Core Abs, Hip Flexors, Quads, Gluts, Calfs, Lower Back, Shoulders

Step 4. Then move your right foot forward, moving it just enough distance to create a 90°angle with your knee and The Box™ sur-face. At the same time, your left knee moves forward dropping down to one inch from The Box™ surface creating a 90° angle

82

LUNGES:

(Step 4 cont.) from your knee to your back right toe. This is the "Down" position.

Step 5. Move back to the Ready or Up position.

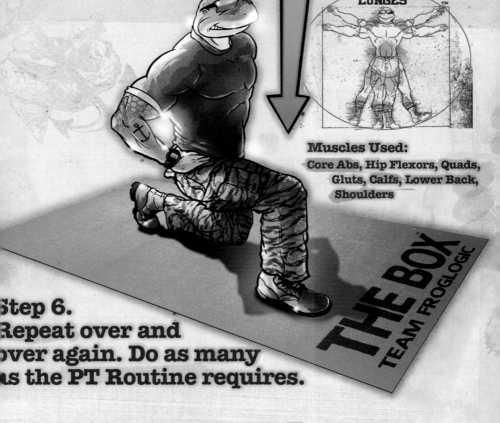

Muscles Used:
Core Abs, Hip Flexors, Quads, Gluts, Calfs, Lower Back, Shoulders

Step 6. Repeat over and over again. Do as many as the PT Routine requires.

Step 7. When Counting make sure to sound off by saying the number "1" after completing the full cycle of the exercise. A full cycle of this exercise is when both feet

LUNGES:

(Step 7 cont.) have moved to the forward or "Down" position and you have returned to the "Up" position. When leading a team of Recruits make sure to give the preparatory commands of "Down" and "Up" in order to make sure everyone is on the same sheet of music. When PTing with a Team, everyone needs to sound off.

Modified Lunges:

If you're having trouble performing the exercise reduce the angle and distance that you move your foot forward and don't drop your knee as far to The Box™ surface. You can also spread your arms out to your sides to help enhance your balance.

Mental Note:

Think about moving through life like climbing a mountain. It takes powerful legs and focused dedication to reach the top. When you're there it's awesome but eventually you've got to come down and begin searching for the next mountain to climb. Up and down. Up and down. That's life. That's Lunges. HOOYAH!

Enhanced Lunges:

Let's start preparing to climb that mountain of life. Push yourself to get better every day. To crush your legs even more go to our website for more Intel on Enhanced Lunges and check out the instructions at DocFrog/PT. OOUUUTT!

84

roglogic™ PT Schedule
unges:

Reps Sets	Mon	Tues	Wed	Thur	Fri
	5	7	10	10	MONSTER MASH
	5	10	7	12	MONSTER MASH
	3	5	3	15	MONSTER MASH

Take a 10 second break between each repetition.
Don't exceed 30 seconds between sets.

DEBRIEF:

_____

_____

_____

_____

_____

_____

_____

_____

_____

FFMK0001 ISSUED BY
TEAMFROGLOGIC HQ

BATTLE 4: CARDIO
MISSION 10 : JUMPING JACKS

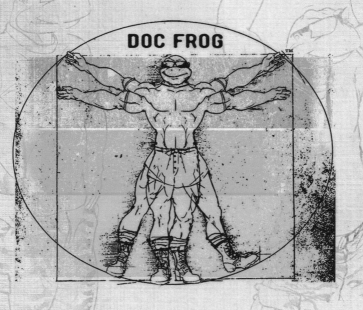

DOC FROG

FFMK0001 ISSUED BY
TEAMFROGLOGIC HQ

CARDIO
MISSION TEN = JUMPING JACKS

Mission Objective: To get your heart pounding and improve your ability to endure the challenges of Mission:Life.

Mental Note:

It's important to remember that it's necessary to give everything you have in order to get better. The harder you push yourself the greater the reward. Now go crush yourself. !!

Nutritional Schedule:

Breakfast –

A piece of French Wheat toast with organic eggs. A half a grapefruit. A glass of almond milk.

Snack 1 –

Some raw carrots. Raw walnuts. Raisins. A big glass of water.

Lunch –

A bean and veggie quesadilla.   A piece of watermelon.
A big glass of water.

Snack 2 –

A green smoothie drink. An organic pear.

Dinner –

Almond crusted chicken fingers. A baked potato. A big glass of water.

INTRO

Giddy up, **Recruit**. It looks like that hammer is beginning to crack against your forged body and fortified intestinal fortitude. Let me hear a loud and thunderous "HOOYAH." Awesome. I believe in you swim buddy, way to fight the good fight. You've just won your third battle, how does that feel? I can only imagine that you must feel like a hard chargin' **PT** animal. The primal voices inside your body, mind and soul are screaming with pride and joy aren't they? I'll bet you feel stronger than ever now, having completed 9 missions. It's amazing when you begin to realize that every repetition makes a difference in shaping your life. With each incredible effort you make, no matter how big or small, you begin to improve your ability to embrace your fears, forge your self-confidence and your commitment toward living the Team Life grows stronger. Roger that!

Well guess what, Recruit? I've saved the best for last, the battle for your Cardio. What's cardio you ask? Great question. Cardio is the wind that helps you sprint for miles. Cardio is the strength that helps you paddle through giant Class 5 rapids. Cardio is the endurance that helps you hike past the tree line in search of waist deep powder when snowboarding.

FFMK0001 ISSUED BY
TEAMFROGLOGIC HQ

INTRO

The strength you've been forging is now needed to propel you towards achieving total mission completion. Each muscle that you've hammered is now ready to be deployed into your toughest battle so far. I know you're ready. So let's crush it!

Jumping Jacks will ignite your body towards fighting that eternal fire in your gut. This timeless exercise has been a staple in the SEAL Teams for decades. I remember doing thousands of these during our infamous Grinder PTs. There is nothing better than sounding off each number with the rest of your team as you close in on 500 straight. Conducting squared away Jacks is the perfect way to get your heart pumping and lungs working hard to forge your Cardio body, mind and spirit. HOOYAH

Come get Some... Fido!

Bring it DOC!

FFMK0001 ISSUED BY
TEAMFROGLOGIC HQ

How to do Jumping Jacks:

Step 1. With The Box™ carefully positioned on the ground, place yourself in the middle of the PT Platform with your feet shoulder width apart and your hands down by your sides. This is the Ready Position.

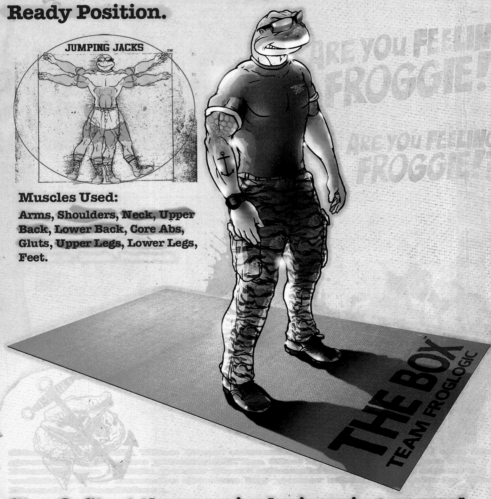

JUMPING JACKS™

Muscles Used:

Arms, Shoulders, Neck, Upper Back, Lower Back, Core Abs, Gluts, Upper Legs, Lower Legs, Feet.

ARE YOU FEELING FROGGIE!

ARE YOU FEELING FROGGIE!

THE BOX™
TEAM FROGLOGIC

Step 2. Start the exercise by jumping upward. While you're in the air, spread your legs apart s

FFMK0001 ISSUED BY
TEAMFROGLOGIC HQ

How to do Jumping Jacks:

(Step 2 cont.) they are about a foot wider than your shoulders. At the same time you're spreading your legs, raise your arms upward and clap your hands together over your head. As your hands clap and you land on the ground you have completed half the exercise. This is the Up Position.

ARE YOU FEELING FROGGIE!?

JUMPING JACKS

Muscles Used:
Arms, Shoulders, Neck, Upper Back, Lower Back, Core Abs, Gluts, Upper Legs, Lower Legs, Feet.

THE BOX
TEAM FROGLOGIC

Step 3. After landing on the ground immediately push yourself into the air again,

How to do Jumping Jacks:

(Step 3 cont.) this time closing your legs and brin-
ing your arms down next to your sides returning to the **Ready or Down Position.** You have
completed one cycle of the exercise or one repetition.

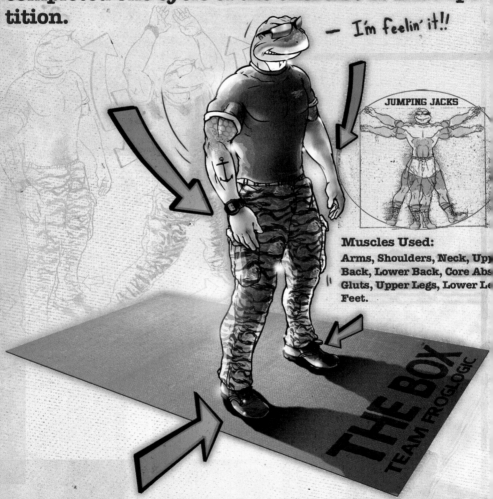

— I'm feelin' it!!

JUMPING JACKS

Muscles Used:
Arms, Shoulders, Neck, Upp
Back, Lower Back, Core Abs
Gluts, Upper Legs, Lower Le
Feet.

THE BOX
TEAM FROGLOGIC

**Step 4. Repeat this again and again, completing
the required number from your PT Routine.**

92

How to do Jumping Jacks:

Step 5. When Counting make sure to sound off by saying the number "1" after completing the full cycle of the exercise. A full cycle of this exercise is complete when your body has returned to the Ready or Down position. When leading a team of Recruits make sure to give the preparatory commands of Up and Down in order to make sure everyone is on the same sheet of music.

Modified Jumping Jacks:

If you are having trouble doing the exercise correctly then switch to doing a "Half Jack." Instead of raising your arms totally over your head simply raise your hands to the same level as your shoulders. You can also make the exercise easier by only spreading your legs shoulder width apart.

Mental Note:

Jumping Jacks are an awesome exercise because it gets your whole body going. Think about the various activities in life where you use everything you've been blessed with. These actions have the biggest impact on improving your physical, mental and spiritual health.

Enhanced Jumping Jacks:

Time to push yourself a little bit harder. Let's get the heart pounding, Recruit. If you want to test your Jumping Jack abilities at the highest level then go to DocFrog.com/PT to find out how.

FFMK0001 ISSUED BY
TEAMFROGLOGIC HQ

Froglogic™ PT Schedule
Jumping Jacks:

Reps / Sets	Mon	Tues	Wed	Thur	Fri
1	25	10	20	50	MONSTER MASH
2	20	30	20	25	MONSTER MASH
3	10	10	20	10	MONSTER MASH

**Take a 10 second break between each repetition.
Don't exceed 30 seconds between sets.**

DEBRIEF:

Don't limit your challenges...

Challenge your Limits!

_____

_____

_____

_____

_____

_____

_____

_____

_____

_____

MISSION 11 : CHASE THE RABBIT

DOC FROG

CARDIO
MISSION ELEVEN : CHASE THE RABBIT

Mission Objective: Increase your cardio capabilities by pushing your limits using all body parts

Mental Note:

Gaining ground in Mission:Life can be misleading sometimes. Often you give a really big effort and feel like you have gone nowhere. It's key to look past the minimal physical distance and embrace the vast amount of ground you've gained mentally and spiritually.

Nutritional Schedule:

Breakfast –

An organic egg white omelet with cheese and spinach. A half grapefruit. A big glass of lemon water.

Snack 1 –

A bowl full of Cacao covered Goji berries. A big glass of almond milk.

Lunch –

A Turkey Burger with bacon, lettuce and tomato on a wheat bun. Organic sweet potato fries. A big glass of water.

Snack 2 –

An almond butter and banana sandwich. A big glass of water.

Dinner –

Fresh line caught trout with steamed vegetables. A big glass of water.

FFMK0001 ISSUED BY
TEAMFROGLOGIC HQ

INTRO

Yeah yeah, Recruit. You're on FIRE! How does it feel? That's what I thought, you're feeling Froggie now aren't cha! HOOYAH. Okay stand by, 'cause you're about to launch right into your next exercise, Chase the Rabbit. Once again your whole body is going to be put to the test. The strength you've forged in your previous battles is going to play a major role in your achieving victory in this mission. Just like in Mission:Life, all the hard work that goes into building your foundation results in major success down the road. That's why I know you're gonna crush it. Because you've crushed yourself so far putting the hard work and positive attitude into the fight. Bravo Zulu teammate. OOUUTT!

Life is hard. That's what makes life so fun. Because when you put forth a real personal and team effort before major operations like big games, tests or tough family situations, the greater strength and perseverance you bring to the mission. Have faith during those long tough training routines that eventually the pain will end and you're gonna come out on top. yeah!

HOOYAH!!

CHASE THE RABBIT:
How to do Chase the Rabbit

Step 1. With The Box™ carefully positioned on the ground, place yourself at one end of The Box.™ Hands down next to your sides. Feet shoulder width apart.

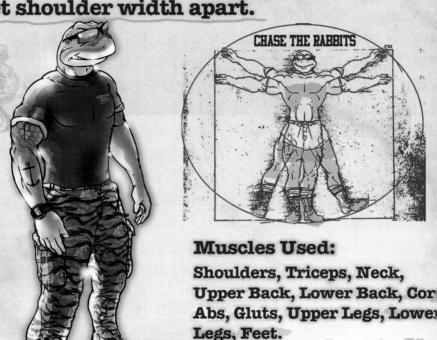

CHASE THE RABBITS

Muscles Used:

Shoulders, Triceps, Neck, Upper Back, Lower Back, Cor Abs, Gluts, Upper Legs, Lower Legs, Feet.

Step 2. Get in the Leaning Rest position. Keeping your back straight and Core

THE BOX™
TEAM FROGLOGIC

FFMK0001 ISSUED BY
TEAMFROGLOGIC HQ

CHASE THE RABBIT:

(Step 2 cont.) Abs tight, spread your legs shoulder width apart balancing on your toes. This is the Ready Position.

Step 3. Your first move is to thrust your left knee forward supported by your toe on The Box™ surface bringing it up underneath your chest. When your knee has reached to the farthest point forward it should remain on the inside of your left elbow. This completes half of the cycle of the exercise.

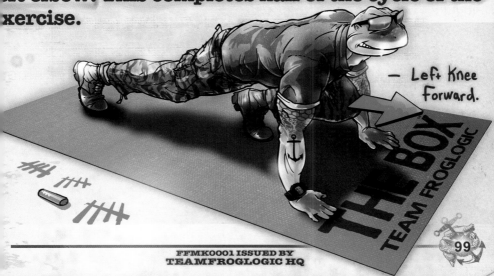

— Left Knee Forward.

CHASE THE RABBIT:

Step 4. Here's where it gets a little tricky. At the same time move your left foot back to its original position and thrust your right knee forward taking its place underneath your chest. You are basically switching places with the other knee and foot.

Left leg back

Right leg forward

This completes one full cycle of the exercise and one repetition.

Right leg back

Left leg forwa

Step 5. Repeat over and over again. Now you're Chasing the Rabbit. ✓

THE BOX
TEAM FROGLOGIC

FFMK0001 ISSUED BY
TEAMFROGLOGIC HQ

HASE THE RABBIT:

tep 6. When Counting make sure to sound ff by saying the number "1" after completng the full cycle of the exercise. Don't let he fatigue of the exercise stop your teammates from sounding off. HOOYAH

Muscles Used:

Shoulders, Triceps, Neck, Upper Back, Lower Back, Core Abs, Gluts, Upper Legs, Lower Legs, Feet.

Modified Chase the Rabbit:

orry Recruits, there is no way to modify hase the Rabbit to make it easier. That's he point. They're hard. Embrace the challenge and push yourself to a new limit.

HOOYAH!!

Mental Note:

Through most of your life you will be chasing something or someone. Whether it's improving your life by going after your dreams or looking or that next great swim buddy to help you live life to its fullest, you ll always be searching. And many times it seems like you're working ally hard and not gaining any ground. Trust me, you're moving Forard with each and every step. The key is to never stop searching for right purpose and the right team. ✓

Awesome!

Enhanced Chase the Rabbit:

Time to drop the Hammer! Faster, stronger, more intense than before. Push yourself and go to DocFrog.com/PT to find out how.

Froglogic™ PT Schedule
Chase The Rabbit:

Reps Sets	Mon	Tues	Wed	Thur	Fri
1	10	20	10	20	MONSTER MASH
2	10	10	30	10	MONSTER MASH
3	10	5	10	20	MONSTER MASH

Take a 10 second break between each repetition.
Don't exceed 30 seconds between sets.

DEBRIEF:

Never throw in the towel... use it to wipe off the sweat!

102

ARE YOU FEELING FROGGIE!?

MISSION 12 : 8 COUNT BODY BUILDERS

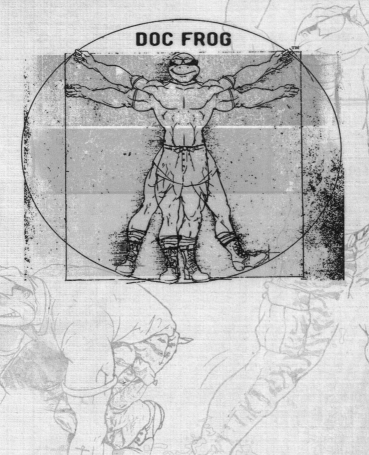
DOC FROG™

FFMK0001 ISSUED BY
TEAMFROGLOGIC HQ

TOTAL BODY

MISSION TWELVE: 8 COUNT BODY BUILDER

Mission Objective: To push yourself further tha[n] you've ever pushed yourself before in Mission: Life. To truly test what your physical, mental and spiritual limits are.

Mental Note:

Here's the deal. 8 counts are the toughest exercise of the whole Manual and that's why I saved them for last. Dig deep and let the reality of what you've already accomplished inspire you to embrac[e] your fear of the exercise, forge your self-confidence to face it head-on and inspire your team to push each other harder than ever before, living the Team Life at its highest possible level.

Nutritional Schedule:

Breakfast –
Two organic eggs over easy. Some bacon. A glass of lemon water.

Snack 1 –
Organic Greek Yogurt with fresh fruit and nuts in it. A big glass of water.

Lunch –
Fish Tacos with papaya salsa and fresh red cabbage. Big glass o[f] water.

Snack 2 –

A banana. A red apple. An orange. A big glass of water.

Dinner –
A giant bowl of whole wheat spaghetti with fresh shrimp. A glass of Almond Milk.

FFMK0001 ISSUED BY
TEAMFROGLOGIC HQ

INTRO

AWESOME job, Recruit. I am so proud of you. You've reached your last mission and done so with flying colors. I know you're feeling hammered but it's time to dig deep. Dig down to the base of your gut where the fear of life can sometimes overwhelm you. Take control and bear hug that fear. Embracing fear will help you forge the self-confidence you need to live the Team Life. You've completed 11 incredibly hard Team Froglogic™ Physical Training missions. Bravo Zulu teammate.

Battle 1: Upper Body- DONE! ✓

Battle 2: Core Abs – DONE! ✓

Battle 3: Lower Body – DONE! ✓

Battle 4 is almost complete. Your body is stronger. Your mind is more focused. Your spirit is like steel. Now for the hardest exercise of all, 8 Count Body Builders. This exercise is the maker and breaker of true Operators. By completing this exercise you are preparing your entire body for any extreme outdoor activity known. This total body crusher does exactly what the name says it does, builds bodies. So get fired up, Recruit, and charge into this last mission with total confidence in who you are and why you're crushing yourself. **HOOYAH**

INTRO

Recruit, being successful in Mission:Life requires the total kit. The Froglogic™ Triad. A healthy body, mind and spirit gives every Team Froglogic™ Operator an advantage when facing the negative insurgency of Old Mr. Murphy. That's why I'm here. To help get you started with your training. Now finish strong, Recruit. Make yourself and your team proud by crushin' your final mission. 8 Count Body Builders ready begin.

How to do 8 Count Body Builders.

Step 1. With The Box™ carefully positioned on th ground, place yourself in the middle of The Box Hands down next to your sides. Feet shoulder width apart. Stand by to forge your physical, mental and spiritual Self-Confidence, totally fo cused and dialed in. This is the Ready or Up position. ✓ I got this!

FFMK0001 ISSUED BY
TEAMFROGLOGIC HQ

How to do 8 Count Body Builders:

This is the Ready or Up position.

8 COUNT BB ™

Muscles Used:
Core Abs, Shoulders, Triceps, Forearms, Hands, Upper Back, Lower back, Neck, Gluts, Upper Legs, Lower Legs, Calfs, Feet.

THE BOX
TEAM FROGLOGIC

ARE YOU FEELING FROGGIE!?

Note: This exercise combines everything you have learned from previous missions. This is an opportunity to reach deep inside and apply all that you have mastered! It's an opportunity to lead your team in a complex and demanding physical challenge. You have come so far! You can do it!

How to do 8 Count Body Builders:

Step 2. Crunch down into a knees-together, squatting position with your palms on the surface of The Box™. This is Count "1."

Squat down

8 COUNT BB™

Muscles Used:
Core Abs, Shoulders, Triceps, Forearms, Hands, Upper Back, Lower back, Neck, Gluts, Upper Legs, Lower Legs, Calfs, Feet.

Step 3. Kick your legs backward, feet together until you're in the Leaning Rest position. This i Count "2."

Kick legs back

THE BOX
TEAM FROGLOGIC

ARE YOU FEELING FROGGIE!?

FFMK0001 ISSUED BY
TEAMFROGLOGIC HQ

Step 4. Move to the Down Push-Up position. Count "3."

come down

_yeah!!

Step 5. Move back into the Leaning Rest Position. Count "4."

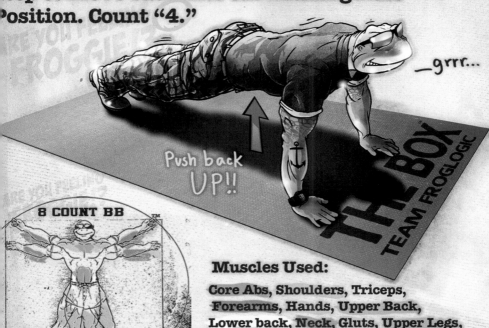

Push back UP!!

_grrr...

8 COUNT BB

Muscles Used:
Core Abs, Shoulders, Triceps, Forearms, Hands, Upper Back, Lower back, Neck, Gluts, Upper Legs, Lower Legs, Calfs, Feet.

Step 6. In a quick movement spread your legs apart one foot wider than your shoulders. This is similar to the **Push-Up Ready Position.** Count "5."

Kick your legs out.

Step 7. Quickly bring your legs back to center and into the **Leaning Rest Position.** Count "6."

Kick your legs Back together.

8 COUNT BB ™

Muscles Used:
Core Abs, Shoulders, Triceps, Forearms, Hands, Upper Back, Lower back, Neck, Gluts, Upper Legs, Lower Legs, Calfs, Feet.

FFMK0001 ISSUED BY
TEAMFROGLOGIC HQ

Step 8. Thrust your legs forward so your knees are tucked underneath your chest and in between your elbows. This is the same as the Count "1" position. This is Count "7."

Thrust your legs forward

ARE YOU FEELING FROGGIE!?

ARE YOU FEELING FROGGIE!?

THE BOX
TEAM FROGLOGIC

8 COUNT BB

Recruit, you're halfway through this exercise! Stay focused...VICTORY is within your grasp!

Muscles Used:
Core Abs, Shoulders, Triceps, Forearms, Hands, Upper Back, Lower back, Neck, Gluts, Upper Legs, Lower Legs, Calfs, Feet.

Step 9. Explode upward into a full Jumping Jack. As you land on your feet, sound off with the repetition number you completed. Sound off with the number "1" or "2" or whatever number you've completed. This is Count "8."

Step 10. Repeat over and over again until you've completed all the required number of 8 Counts in your PT Routine.

THE BOX
TEAM FROGLOGIC

FFMK0001 ISSUED BY
TEAMFROGLOGIC HQ

Step 11. Counting. Because you are doing an 8 Count Body Builder you should be counting out loud as you complete each phase of the exercise. Example: "1,2,3,4,5,6,7,1." Next Rep.: "1,2,3,4,5,6,7,2." Next Rep.: "1,2,3,4,5,6,7,3."

Modified 8 Count Body Builders:

Once again, Recruit, there is no easier way to do 8 Counts. This is a full body exercise designed to test your progress on all your other exercises. This is a huge challenge for all physically fit people. That's why it's critical for you to do each part of the exercise with total focus and determination. HOOYAH

Mental Note:

When you're confronted with extremely difficult challenges in your Mission:Life you can't quit. Nothing great in life comes easy. Achieving your dreams takes tons of hard work and sacrifice to be better at anything you want to achieve. When you are feeling the Hammer most, that's when you have to dig the deepest in your body, mind and spirit to push past the pain of the moment and let your unwavering faith in yourself embrace your fear, forge your self-confidence and live the Team Life. Remember, the only easy day was yesterday. Never Quit! HOOYAH!! :)

I am so fired up that you've pushed your self this far, Recruit. Way to go. Time to go all the way. HOOYAH. www.DocFrog.com/PT

Froglogic™ PT Schedule
8 Count Body Builders:

Reps Sets	Mon	Tues	Wed	Thur	Fri
1	5	10	10	5	MONSTER MASH
2	5	5	15	20	MONSTER MASH
3	5	5	5	10	MONSTER MASH

Take a 10 second break between each repetition.
Don't exceed 30 seconds between sets.

DEBRIEF:

_____

_____

_____

_____

_____

_____

_____

_____

_____

_____

Quitters Never win.
Winners Never QUIT!!

FFMK0001 ISSUED BY
TEAMFROGLOGIC HQ

Debrief

HOOYAH Recruits! Bravo Zulu to you and the awesome effort you just made to complete this Field Manual. I know that you're already feeling a thousand times stronger physically, mentally and spiritually. It's important to remember that forging yourself into a squared away Team Froglogic™ Operator requires a lot of motivation and hard work. Nothing worth achieving comes easy and the only easy day was yesterday. If you commit yourself and your life to embracing fear, forging self-confidence and living a Team Life, you WILL realize your dreams. ✳

You've begun this process by accepting my challenge to complete 4 Battles and 12 Missions. I got you focused on four different fitness operations in my Physical Training Manual. In Battle 1 you started to embrace strengthening your Upper Body. I know it was tough doing all 3 Missions that include Push-Ups, Wide Grip Push-Ups and Diamond Push-Ups, but don't you feel stronger? You bet your upper body you do. Your upper body got hammered but now you're ready to climb, push, pull or lift anything that helps you grow stronger. I'm super proud of you because you pushed past being tired and pulled yourself up to complete all your Upper Body missions. Well done, Recruit. ✓

FFMK0001 ISSUED BY
TEAMFROGLOGIC HQ

In Battle 2, I got you squared away by strengthening your Core Abs. These muscles are critical to your body structure and intestinal fortitude. These exercises are not easy, Recruit. In fact Crunches, Knee Up Outer Obliques and 4 Count Flutter Kicks can make even the best operators struggle and want to quit. However, every time you pick yourself up off the floor and get back on The Box to finish the PT Schedule, you win. That's right Recruit, by completing each part of every mission no matter how long it takes, you win physical, mentally and spiritually. And it pays to be a winner.

For Battle 3, I hammered your Lower Body and turned your legs into forged steel. Didn't I? More like spaghetti noodles. Don't worry Recruit, you're gonna get strong. By accepting these three missions, Lunges, Calf Raises and Air Squats, you began to understand how important a strong base is when participating in extreme sports or Navy SEAL exercises. Mission:Life has us running all the time. Without fortifying your lower body, you'll never be able to chase down your dreams. Trust me Recruit, putting the time in to develop a rock hard lower body helps you prepare for the ultra-marathon of life. Mission:Life never ends, so never stop strengthening your legs for the long road ahead. March on!

FFMK0001 ISSUED BY
TEAMFROGLOGIC HQ

attle 4 was a crusher. Cardio PT at its finest. I know I ammered the snot out of you during these missions, ut you finished strong. HOOYAH! Jumping Jacks, hase The Rabbit and 8 Count Body Builders will umble the best of us, Recruit. My Team and I perform ese missions all the time to test our resolve just like tested yours. Well guess what, you didn't let me down. m so proud of you! Pushing yourself past your known mits on a regular basis will not only help you become ealthier but also teach you what you're really made of. opefully you now understand that in the face of any eal world challenge, like doing twenty straight 8 Count ody Builders, you know that no matter how tired you t you have what it takes to complete the Mission. ravo Zulu Recruit!

OOYAH! Are you feeling Froggie? Well are ya? It's ry important that you feel proud of yourself for mpleting this Froglogic™ Field Manual for Kids. All of at Team Froglogic™ are totally proud of you and your am. You're on your way to becoming a critical ember of Team Froglogic™. By completing all of the issions in this PT Manual, you've made the focused cision to strengthen your body, mind and spirit. In der to operate at an elite level during your Mission: fe, you need to constantly work on your Froglogic™ riad. Doing a little bit every day will help you embrace ar, forge self-confidence and live a Team Life.

Living a healthy well-balanced life empowers you to achieve your dreams, just as long as you NEVER QUIT and you're willing to work hard with your teammates. Thank you Recruit, and I look forward to hearing from you on our website, www.DocFrog.com. God bless you and your team.

Your new Swim Buddy, stay motivated!

Doc Frog™

FFMK0001 ISSUED BY
TEAMFROGLOGIC HQ

PT Evolutions

HOOYAH Recruits, you've finished perfecting all the individual missions. You're feeling Froggie, and ready to test yourself physically, mentally and spiritually. It's time to get hammered and start doing your Team Frog-logic PT Evolutions. Good luck and train hard. *

PT Evolution #1 ✓

Monday	Push-Ups Reps	Crunches Reps	Lunges Reps	Jumping Jacks Reps
Set 1	2,4,6	10,10	5	25
Set 2	6,4,2	10,5	5	25
Set 3	2,4,6	2,4,6	5	10

PT Evolution #2 ✓

Tuesday	Wide Grip Push-Ups Reps	Knee Up Outer Obliques Reps	Calf Raises Reps	Chase the Rabbit Reps
Set 1	3,4,6	Lt 10, Rt 10	25	20
Set 2	5,4,2	Lt 5, Rt 5	15	10
Set 3	3,4,6	Lt 3, Rt 3	5	5

FFMK0001 ISSUED BY
TEAMFROGLOGIC HQ

PT Evolution #3 ✓

Wednesday	Diamond Push-Ups Reps	4 Count Flutter Kicks Reps	Air Squats Reps	8 Count Body Builders Reps
Set 1	4,4,4	10	10	10
Set 2	4,4,4	15	30	15
Set 3	4,4,4	10	10	5

PT Evolution #4 ✓

Thursday	Push-Ups Reps	Crunches Reps	Lunges Reps	Jumping Jacks Reps
Set 1	5,5,5,5	10,20	10	50
Set 2	3,3,3,3	20,10	12	25
Set 3	2,2,2,2	20,10,15	15	10

PT Evolution #5 ✓

Friday	Push-Ups Reps	Knee Up Outer Obliques Reps	Calf Raises Reps	Chase the Rabbit Reps
Set 1	10	Lt 5 Rt 5	10	10
Set 2	10	Lt 20 Rt 20	30	30
Set 3	5,5,5	Lt 5 Rt 5	10	10

FFMK0001 ISSUED BY TEAMFROGLOGIC HQ

PT Evolution #6 ✓

Monday	Wide Grip Push-Ups Reps	Crunches Reps	Air Squats Reps	Jumping Jacks Reps
Set 1	4,6,8	15,15	25	20
Set 2	6,5,4	10,15	15	20
Set 3	5,6,3	2,4,6,4,2	5	20

PT Evolution #7 ✓

Tuesday	Push-Ups Reps	Knee Up Outer Obliques Reps	Calf Raises Reps	Chase the Rabbit Reps
Set 1	10	Lt 5 Rt 5	10	10
Set 2	10	Lt 20 Rt 20	30	30
Set 3	5,5,5	Lt 5 Rt 5	10	10

PT Evolution #8 ✓

Wednesday	Diamond Push-Ups Reps	Flutter Kicks Reps	Lunges Reps	8 Count Body Builders Reps
Set 1	10	5	5	5
Set 2	10	10	5	5
Set 3	5,5,5	5	3	5

PT Evolution Monster Mash Example:

Monster MASH#1	Push-Ups Mon Wed Reps	Crunches Tue Thur Reps	Calf Raises Mon Tue Reps	Chase the Rabbit Wed Thur Reps
Set 1	2,4,6 10	15,15 10,20	10 25	10 25
Set 2	6,4,2 10	10,15 20,10	10 15	30 10
Set 3	2,4,6 5,5,5	2,4,6,4,2 20,10,15	7 5	10 20

FFMK0001 ISSUED BY
TEAMFROGLOGIC HQ

Glossary

Abs – Your abdominal muscles.

Activated Core – The process of tightening your abdominal muscles just prior to beginning your exercise or activity.

Air Ops – Air Operations.

Ancient Mesopotamia – An area in the Middle East that was considered the cradle of civilization from 3100 BC to around 539 BC.

Are you Feeling Froggie?™ – Doc Frog's variant of a Navy SEAL motto and question that means, are you truly up for the challenge?

Attention to the Details – A key concept within Team Froglogic™ that instills the perpetual need to pay close attention to the little things that make the difference between winning and losing.

Battle – A concept and action that puts two opponents against each other. In your case for example, Battle 1 – Upper Body, pits you and your existing strength capabilities against Doc Frog's Physical Training Manual.

Bravo Zulu – A Naval Signal that means "Well Done."

Big Missions – These are the Missions that include your big goals, big challenges and big dreams. You will achieve your Big Missions.

Cardio – Exercise concepts that include all your muscles and body parts designed to enhance your heart and lung capacity. Exercises that help you develop strength, endurance and the ability to persevere in life.

Comfort Zones – The place in your mind where you make excuses in order to not hammer yourself with hard work.

Core Abs – Your core muscles or abdominal muscles locate in your stomach region. These are the muscles that gener ate positive structural form while doing any extreme activities or just maintaining good posture.

Daily Ops – These are the Little Ops that take place every day. Successfully completing these leads to total success i the Big Ops or Big Missions.

Demo – To demonstrate something or a demonstration.

Debrief – A specific action that takes place after an operation where all participants discuss and record the lessons learned from the Op, particularly their failures.

Dig Deep – A motivational statement used often at Team Froglogic™ that helps operators dig down deep in their Fro logic™ Triad to find the will to succeed.

Dive Ops – Special Operations that mean Dive Operations.

Doc Frog™ – An awesome Special Operations, Superhero. Team Leader at Team Froglogic™. A dedicated operator an committed swim buddy to his teammates.

Embrace Your Fear – A Team Froglogic™ core concept that helps recruits and operators remember that fear is a positive thing in their lives.

Enhanced – Making something better or tougher.

FFMK0001 ISSUED BY
TEAMFROGLOGIC HQ

Explosive – A mindset or energy boost that helps operators complete their missions.

Fire in the Gut – A Navy SEAL motto that expresses the internal, burning desire to be better at everything in their lives.

Forge Self Confidence – A Team Froglogic™ core concept that helps recruits and operators remember that every day is a day they need to strengthen their Self-Confidence.

Field Manual – A book used to help recruits and operators learn new important techniques and training concepts to become more successful in Mission:Life.

Four Count Counting System – A system of counting during exercises that enhances the strengthening process. Example: "1,2,3,1" then "1,2,3,2," next "1,2,3,3" and finally "1,2,3,4."

FLC – Froglogic Concepts, LLC

FFMK™ – Froglogic Field Manuals for Kids™

Froglogic™ – (frog-lojik), n.v. 1. A motivational philosophy that strengthens a person's body, mind and spirit and perpetually inspires that individual's desire to embrace fear, forge their Self-Confidence and Live The Team Life. 2. A three-part motivational training program. (Part 1) – Accepting 5 Life Missions to Embrace Fear and begin using your fear as a positive productive piece of motivational gear. (Part 2) – Accepting 8 Life Missions into your lifestyle in order to forge your Self-Confidence. (Part 3) –

Over 70 years of UDT/ Navy SEAL operations, training and elite lifestyle performance, expanded by the Overall Special Operations Mindset.

Froglogic™ Concepts, LLC – A Motivational Entertainment Company. Company Motto – "Motivational Media That Matters."

Froglogic™ PT Schedule – A basic physical training schedu for recruits to follow as they learn to perfect the exercise

Froglogic™ Triad – A concept that operators on Team Froglogic™ are totally focused on as they pursue developing a healthy body, mind and spirit.

Froglogic™ Field Manuals for Kids – Field Manuals designe to help kids learn to Embrace Fear, Forge Self-Confidence and Live the Team Life. These easy to use, portable training guides will help children achieve total mission success. The first of these Field Manuals is Doc Frog's™ Physical Training Manual.

Frogman – A term originally used to describe members of the Underwater Demolition Teams during WWII. A term used to describe Doc and his fellow frog brothers dedicate to getting kids squared away.

Get Squared Away™ – When you focus on getting your life organized by developing your body, mind and spirit to become a healthy, well-balanced operator.

Get Some – A phrase that Team Froglogic™ operators shout out to each other during total hammer sessions.

FFMK0001 ISSUED BY
TEAMFROGLOGIC HQ

o Big – Another fired up phrase that helps operators suck up and accept the truly hard challenges in Mission:Life.

$_2$O Delivery Apparatus – Water bottle. ✓

ammer – When you push yourself beyond your known mits and accept the reality that improving your body, ind and spirit takes tons of hard work.

ealthy Fuel – The proper nutritional food and drink that nhances your ability to be successful in anything you ttempt.

ydration – Drinking water or liquids that help you ecover and maintain proper fluid levels in your body.

ydrate or Die – A Special Operations saying that inspires perators to stay hydrated during missions.

OOYAH – The Navy SEAL motivational "War Cry." A ar Cry has been used for thousands of years by driven arrior poets to inspire themselves and their teammates stay in the fight of life at all times.

tel – Useful pieces of information that help us make good ntelligent decisions towards achieving our dreams in ission:Life.

tel Words – Words Doc Frog™ uses to help explain key oncepts and points in his Field Manuals.

ISS – An acronym that means Keep It Simple Stupid. his means that you should not overcomplicate things hen you're learning the basics or planning for Big and ittle Missions.

127

Kit – A special operators gear.

Little Ops – These are the little tasks you perform during your daily routine. However, performing these ops correctly is critical in achieving your overall missions or Big Goals.

Lessons Learned – Critical life lessons you've learned from watching, living and feeling the impact of the world around you.

Leaning Rest – This is the starting position when conducting Push-Ups.

Live The Team Life – A Team Froglogic core concept that helps recruits and operators remember that every day is a day they need to commit their lives towards living a team-oriented lifestyle.

Loud and Thunderous – A way to express the sheer joy and excitement of getting hammered.

Lower Body – All the muscles that comprise the lower portions of your body.

Mental Fortitude – Extreme focus and mental commitment that happens when using Froglogic to succeed in Mission:Life.

Mental Note – A key concept that Doc Frog wants you to think about when conducting each mission.

Mental PT – Mental exercise. You've got to build your brain like your brawn.

FFMK0001 ISSUED BY
TEAMFROGLOGIC HQ

Mental Task – A task that you give yourself to execute in your mind.

Mission:Life – The epic journey that begins when you're born and ends when you move on into the afterlife.

Modified – A term used in the Field Manual that means altering the exercise in order to perform the basics to perfection.

Monster Mash – When a recruit or operator combines PT schedules to create a total hammer session workout that challenges every aspect of your body, mind and spirit.

Motivational Music Delivery Apparatus – Anything that pumps music into your soul.

Muscle Burn – That slight burn and fatigue your muscles feel when pushing yourself past your limits.

Negative Insurgency – The perpetual negativity that society by and large generates as a result of large groups of unmotivated people breaking others down physically, mentally and spiritually because they aren't happy with their lives.

Never Quit – A Navy SEAL creed that drives them to Embrace Fear, Forge Self-Confidence and Live the Team Life every day of their lives.

Nutritional Schedule – A day and night's worth of menu suggestions to help prepare you to start putting the right fuel in your body.

Old Mr. Murphy – The evil leader of the negative insurgency, always lurking behind the shadows desperately trying to undermine your ability to be successful in Mission:Life.

Operator – A totally squared away member of the Special Operations community or Team Froglogic.™

PT – Physical Training

PT Platform – The Box˝ or any sufficient place to conduct PT.

Real World – Tough life experiences that teach real lesson

Recovery – The critical period after conducting any type of mission during life. This is the focused time for all operators to recuperate and begin to prepare physically, mentally and spiritually for their next mission.

Reps – Repetitions. The number of times you perform the exercises listed in your PT Schedule.

Rest – The critical time after a mission or operation when the recruit or operator needs to totally shut down his body mind and spirit.

Ruck – An operator's backpack.

Sets – The combined group of repetitions.

Sound Off – When a recruit or operator calls out during PT

Special Operations – Classified missions that entail the hardest, most challenging operations in the world.

FFMK0001 ISSUED BY
TEAMFROGLOGIC HQ

piritual Challenges – Deep moral, ethical and soulful
hallenges all operators face while trying to succeed in
Mission:Life.

piritual Health – Strong, focused faith in your self and
our team.

uck it Up – A term used by operators to each other that
eans for the recipient to dig deep and finish strong.

wim Buddy – A person who you can absolutely count on
help you maintain your mission focus in life no matter
hat negative insurgency you both may face. Someone
tally committed to living the Team Life.

eam Froglogic™ – Doc Frog™ and his group of highly moti-
ated special operations, superheroes. Their mission is to
elp kids around the world Embrace Fear, Forge Self-
onfidence and Live the Team Life.

eam Life – An operator's total commitment toward living
team-oriented lifestyle in every aspect of his or her life.

he Only Easy Day was Yesterday – A Navy SEAL motto
at lets operators know that nothing in life is easy, except
day already completed.

he Box™ – The Team Froglogic™ PT Platform

S Navy SEAL – A Special Operations commando who
xcels in the Sea, up in the Air and on Land.

NSAT – Unsatisfactory.

pper Body – All the muscles that comprise the upper
ortions of your body.

Vigorous Activity – Hard core physical activity that lasts for at least 60 minutes.

Warm-Up – A slow gradual process that prepares the body for vigorous activity.

FFMK0001 ISSUED BY
TEAMFROGLOGIC HQ

Editor's Note

I have had the pleasure of knowing David Rutherford for many years. When I learned he was going to enlist in the Navy with the goal of becoming a SEAL, I was excited for him. However, I was aware of the physically demanding and mentally challenging training that would be required of him to achieve his goal, and I couldn't help but feel anxious. At the same time, I had no doubt that David had the strong character and commitment to Team that is required to become a SEAL. I knew he would never give up. Despite suffering various injuries and setbacks, David persevered and realized his dream of becoming a Navy SEAL.

During David's travels with the SEALs and then as an International Training Specialist, he witnessed children in Afghanistan and other places whose countries had been at war their entire lives, and whose innocence had been shattered through no fault of their own. He dreamed of mentoring children and helping them develop a philosophy that would help them cope with the extreme hardships they were facing.

Much closer to home, David was alarmed at the number of children who lack physical fitness and good nutrition as a part of their daily lives. According to the President's Council on Fitness, Sports & Nutrition, children and adolescents should get 60 minutes or more of physical activity daily. The reality is that children spend more than 7-1/2 hours a day in front of a screen (e.g., TV, videogames and computers), and only one in three children are physically active every day. Data from 2009-2010 indicates that about 12.5 million (16.9%) children and adolescents are obese. According to the American Heart Association, obesity is causing a broad range of health problems among children today that previously weren't seen until adulthood. There are also psychological effects: obese children are more prone to low self-esteem, negative body image and depression.

It was clear that Team Froglogic™ needed to step up to the plate. We went BIG, and are excited to introduce our coo superhero, Doc Frog™ In his first Field Manual, Navy SEAL PT for Kids, Doc™ embraces his mission to inspire and educate kids with a fun way to become healthier, physically, mentally and spiritually. With Brian Kalt's beautiful illustrations, Doc Frog™ demonstrates step-by-step instructions for strengthening the upper body, core abs and lower body, adding cardio as an important part an effective fitness program. Doc Frog's™ Recruits are challenged to incorporate physical training and good nutrition as an integral part of their everyday lives, whi sharpening their mental focus and emphasizing the importance of living a Team Life.

The creation of Doc Frog's™ Field Manual for Kids has bee a labor of love for all of us at Team Froglogic™ I truly believe this Field Manual will be a life-changer for kids who embrace Doc Frog's™ challenge and begin shaping th success of their future by strengthening their bodies, minds and spirits.

P.S. And for all you kids who read the Editor's Notes,

HOOYAH!!

Kathleen "Kat" Goodrich

Kathleen Goodrich
Editor / Team Member

For more information please visit Doc Frog™
and the rest of Team Froglogic™ at

www.DocFrog.com

FFMK0001 ISSUED BY
TEAMFROGLOGIC HQ

FINAL DEBRIEF:

HooYah!
Recruit!!
You Made it.
DOO is super
proud of you!

FINAL DEBRIEF cont.:

FINAL DEBRIEF cont.: